Decade of Despair

Winnebago County during the Great Depression, 1929–1939

Werner E. Braatz and Thomas J. Rowland

University Press of America,® Inc.
Lanham · Boulder · New York · Toronto · Plymouth, UK

Copyright © 2009 by
University Press of America,® Inc.
4501 Forbes Boulevard
Suite 200
Lanham, Maryland 20706
UPA Acquisitions Department (301) 459-3366

Estover Road
Plymouth PL6 7PY
United Kingdom

All rights reserved
Printed in the United States of America
British Library Cataloging in Publication Information Available

Library of Congress Control Number: 2009924647

ISBN: 978-0-7618-4640-6
ISBN: 0-7618-4640-9

♾™ The paper used in this publication meets the minimum requirements of American National Standard for Information Sciences—Permanence of Paper for Printed Library Materials, ANSI Z39.48-1992

Table of Contents

Preface	v
Chapter One: 1929: The Crash	1
Chapter Two: 1930: The Onset of Depression	11
Chapter Three: 1931: The Depression Deepens	21
Chapter Four: 1932: The Depths of Depression	29
Chapter Five: 1933: The Federal Government Weighs In	39
Chapter Six: 1934: New Directions in Relief	55
Chapter Seven: 1935-1937: Putting People to Work	71
Chapter Eight: 1937-1939: The Woes of Labor	89
Epilogue: Hope on the Horizon	107
Index	111

Preface

On a cold drizzly day, March 4, 1929, the newly elected president of the United States delivered his inaugural address to the nation. Although he cautioned that there were "some causes for concern," the bulk of his remarks on the progress of the nation was glowing. "We have reached a higher degree of comfort and security," he crowed, "than ever existed in the history of the world." Progress was so thorough, Hoover claimed that "we are steadily building a new race--a new civilization great in its own attainments." Never, perhaps, was a president more right and more wrong at the same time. Seven months later this near-utopian vision lay shattered in ruins. The Great Depression, which made its arrival known in October 1929, sundered the prosperity and general optimism Hoover had hailed earlier that year. The next decade would be marked by impoverishment and despair.[1]

The deleterious effects of the Great Depression were felt in virtually every corner of the nation. Winnebago County in the state of Wisconsin was certainly no exception. At the very moment Herbert Hoover was waxing eloquent over the sound state of the nation's economy, Winnebago County, a largely urban region in the state's Fox River Valley, was enjoying its own slice of economic prosperity. Factories, mills and plants, including the dominant and traditional ones of paper making and lumber milling, were reporting extraordinarily high capacities in production. Unemployment was practically non-existent; if someone was not working it was his or her own choice. Retailers rejoiced in the generous consumer spending of the day. Agricultural concerns in the county may not have been swept up in the general exhilaration of the period, but, on the whole, Winnebago county was a good place to live. All this changed in late October 1929. For a full decade Winnebago county was forced to struggle with the ravages of an economy that had been eviscerated by the onset of financial chaos initiated by the collapse of Wall Street on those fateful autumn days in 1929.

This modest study, then, is an attempt to come to terms with the character of that struggle in Winnebago County between the years 1929 and 1939. Any attempt to fully address the entire spectrum of the impact the Great Depression had upon any place, even a localized one like Winnebago County, is fraught with inadequacy and injustice. Hence, this work seeks to understand the extent of the industrial collapse in the county and to understand why in some cities the downturn was more precipitous than in others. The misfortune of industry begs the essential question--what effect did it have on employment? This, too, is a large part of the focus of this study. Massive unemployment by necessity imposed extraordinary demands on poor relief structures and this work examines how local jurisdictions tried to handle it on their own until all of their resources dried up.

Another integral part of this study addresses the scope and organization of federal, state, and county government efforts to assume responsibility for providing relief, most often through subsidized work projects, as well as measures taken to revitalize the local economy. It is also of vital interest to address the lives of those put out of work by the Great Depression. How did they cope with both the lack of resources but the debilitating stress of unemployment? In fact, this study attempts to put a human face on the challenges and struggles that ordinary people throughout the county had to confront in this decade of despair. Hopefully, then, this work will provide an insight, perhaps a snapshot, of life in Winnebago County during the Great Depression.

The authors gratefully acknowledge that no undertaking such as this study could be completed without the assistance of key individuals. We would like to thank Kelly L. Bezio, doctoral candidate in English and Comparative Literature at the University of North Carolina, for her painstaking review of research documents and materials in the State Historical Society of Wisconsin. Paul Stellflug, a teacher at Oshkosh West High School, conducted interviews dealing with the local experience during the Prohibition and Depression eras while an undergraduate at the University of Wisconsin-Oshkosh, and we are indebted to him for their use in this study. Joshua Ranger, archivist at the University of Wisconsin-Oshkosh, along with his staff were enormously helpful in addressing every manner of inquiry. Lane Earns, Provost and Vice-Chancellor of the university, provided welcomed encouragement and timely advice.

Finally, the authors would like to dedicate this study to the honor and memory of Joseph P. Starr, who, prior to his passing in October 2006, spearheaded the research for this study and guided a couple of the early chapters through to first drafts. Dr. Starr, an Associate Professor of History at the University of Wisconsin-Oshkosh was a long time colleague and dear friend of Werner Braatz and an accomplished teacher and scholar. This completed study is but a small tribute to a learned and gracious man.

Werner E. Braatz
Thomas J. Rowland
Oshkosh, Wisconsin
September 2008

---

1. *The Inaugural Address of Herbert Hoover, March 4, 1939 in* http://www.yal.edu/lawweb/avalon/presiden/inaug/hoover.html, p. 1.

Chapter 1

1929: The Crash

The worst disaster in the Wall Street stock market began in earnest in the third week of October 1929. There had been sharp declines during the previous six weeks but on Monday, October 21, there occurred one of the greatest selling frenzies in the market's long history.[1] Leading shares tumbled $5 to $35. Selling orders poured in from all parts of the county and from abroad. On Tuesday the trend continued. Thousands of small traders who failed to meet their margins were sold out suffering heavy losses. Wednesday was no better. There were scenes of wild confusion as prices continued to plunge. The ticker tape fell more than half an hour behind market activity and traders were frightened into bewildering selling when word reached brokerage offices that prices on the floor of the stock exchange were several dollars below the quotations being printed on the tape. By the time the market closed that day the value of shares had fallen by $4 billion. Thursday, to be remembered as Black Thursday, was still worse. Almost 13 million shares had been traded when the closing gong sounded. The public was fascinated by the drama:

> ...thousands of sightseers, drawn by the shrieks and groans emanating from the Stock Exchange Building, invaded the district causing terrific traffic jams and forcing city authorities to send extra police to the area. James N. Rosenberg, a Wall Street attorney and spare-time artist, drew a shocking sketch of the district on Black Thursday, one filled with imaginary skyscrapers collapsing, as if in an earthquake, upon a horrified mob in the street. "I was bursting with emotion that day," Rosenberg recalled, "...it seemed like the end of America."[2]

On Friday, October 25, calm returned when stock price levels briefly stabilized. This was accomplished through the intervention of powerful banking interests who formed a pool to place huge buying orders, worth $20 to $30 million, in an attempt to bolster the market and calm fears--until they themselves could get out. Once again thousands of gawkers invaded the district in hopes of seeing an unusual and rewarding sight: rich men losing lots of money.

1

A jittery weekend passed. Those few who still retained a strong faith in the strength of the Stock Exchange were assured by President Herbert Hoover that the panic of the preceding week had been a temporary phenomenon and that the general condition of American business was strong and sound.[3]

But these assertions had no effect on the market when it opened its doors on Monday, October 28. Prices continued to plummet and by the end of the day the value of shares had fallen by $14 billion. Then came Tuesday, October 29, the most devastating single day in the market's history. By its end, shares had fallen nearly $26 billion and the United States had been launched into the most calamitous financial recession in its history.[4]

At the time few in Wisconsin's Winnebago County realized the magnitude of what had happened and most people, still hopeful, agreed with the soothing words of the *Oshkosh Northwestern* which that fateful day of October 29 asserted:

> This is a big county and all the factors that make it great are still at its command--brains, inventive genius, natural resources, unexcelled transportation facilities, adequate capital, level-headed government and a sound and tested banking system. On that account no occasion for anyone to worry except the gambler who bets his money on the market ups and downs of prices.[5]

As we know now the paper was wildly optimistic. During the next four years the national income was to fall by more than one-half (from $87.8 billion to $40.2 billion) and the gross national product from $104.4 billion to $56 billion.[6]

Did no one see it coming? Yes, there were a few. In the autumn of 1927, for example, Frank J. Weber, general secretary of the Milwaukee Federated Trades Council, predicted that unemployment nation-wide would become a problem toward the end of 1929 and then become quite severe for a two-year period.[7] There were other signs. In 1928, business failures in Wisconsin alone numbered 403 firms with total debts of $6,062,554;[8] in the same year the cost for general outdoor relief in Wisconsin amounted to $1,200,000.[9] By the summer of 1929 conservative bankers and financiers were also pointing out that consumer spending, production and employment were declining throughout the country.[10] Among them was Joseph P. Kennedy, a Wall Street maven, who was increasingly alarmed about entry into the market of amateur investors who knew nothing about its arcane workings and therefore began to sell his stocks. He told associates that "when he heard his hotel shoe shine boy dispensing market advice, he knew the time had come to get out."[11]

Although there were sufficient warnings, far too many people believed that things were going to get better. An editorial in the *Daily News Times* of Neenah on September 23, scarcely a month before the crash, recaptured the general feeling of economic well being in Winnebago County. "Probably there is no surer index of economic security and prosperity of the people of the United States to be found, than the amount and number of their savings," it declared. In support of its assertion, the editorial referred to the Bank of Manhattan Company's, The

Greatest Family in the World, which dealt with the financial statistics of big business and families. "The little book," the editor explained, "presents striking proof of our increasing economic prosperity." The editorial proceeded to review the statistics: from 1923 to 1929 savings accounts increased from $30 million to $53 million and the amount of savings from $12 billion to $28 billion, an increase of over 75 percent. The conclusion to this analysis was hortatory:

> It takes real prosperity to bring about such an unprecedented increase in savings. This gives evidence that Americans are making provision for the future. These figures show that the commercial and industrial life of the country is being established on a sound and practically unassailable foundation.[12]

In 1929, Winnebago County, the seventh largest in Wisconsin, with an area of 449 square miles, had a population of 76,600, having grown by 13,000 since the last census taken in 1920. The native white population was nearly 68,000; the foreign-born came to 8,600. There were only 60 African-Americans; other groups came to about 200.[13] Of the inhabitants, the Germans dominated and still clung to their culture, although it was gradually eroding and being absorbed by the process of Americanization. For example, in 1928, at Peace Lutheran Church, the largest Protestant parish in Oshkosh, 27 children were confirmed in German and 25 in English. The next year, however, only 10 of 28 were confirmed in German.[14]

Winnebago County was overwhelmingly urban; the number of farmers--owners, tenants and laborers--was small, about 4,000. Oshkosh, the county seat was the largest city with a population of about 40,000. Of these 18,000 were born of foreign parents and 10,500 of families where only one parent was native-born. Oshkosh, dubbed the "Sawdust City," was incorporated in 1853 and grew rapidly because it was at the southern end of the white pine timber watershed and the streams and rivers fed the cut logs into the basin near Lake Butte des Morts. When the railroad came in 1859, Oshkosh became the point where the timber was sawed and loaded on trains to go to eastern markets. By 1900, however, local timber had virtually disappeared but the sawmills began making woodworking machinery and metal products; soon generators and motor parts and a metal industry was founded.[15]

Neenah and Menasha were the next biggest cities in the county, each having about 9,000 inhabitants in 1930. Of the two, Menasha, whose population had grown by 33% since the census of 1920, was the most civically ambitious. Keen to attract and keep businesses, Menasha, for example, agreed to refund the taxes paid in 1928 by the Menasha Paper Mill Company in order to retain the firm in the city. The same action was repeated for 1929 when Menasha refunded $3,829.74 to the company for taxes paid.[16] By 1929, the existing city slogan, "Menasha the City of Paper and Pails Always to the Front and Never Fails," was considered hackneyed and the citizens were asked to select a new one. A contest was held and the judges chose, "Menasha the Industrial City." This became the official salutation by resolution of the mayor and the common council.[17] The new slogan definitely lacked the panache of the old one. Menasha had its critics too. In March 1931, for instance, Frank Buckley, an investigator for the Prohibition Bureau, reported that "Menasha is very wet. It houses a rough, foreign element that creates a liquor, prostitution and gambling market." He was immediately rebuked by Michael Riley, the local congressman, who pointed out that although it was true the ancestry of Menasha's population was 80% German and Polish, "Menasha is in no sense a foreign city; it is an American city, a patriotic city, and a city of deep religious and moral sentiment."[18]

Almost 30,000 in the county worked in industry. Paper mills and woodworking companies, which by this time obtained their lumber from elsewhere, were the largest with about 6,300 employees, of whom over 900 were women. About 1,700 people worked in the building industry and about 1,100 in iron and steel. Nearly 3,600, including about 900 women, were in the wholesale and retail trades.[19]

By no means was prosperity universal in Winnebago County before the crash. In 1928, there was enough poverty to require the State Department of Public Relief to expend $104,243 in the county.[20] Municipal agencies occasionally made small attempts to relieve the situation. Around Thanksgiving in 1928, the Oshkosh Recreation Department organized a show to be given in a local cinema at which the price of admission was a food donation to the poor. Three tons of food were collected.[21] As well, the amount spent by the county required under the Aid to Dependent Children's Law was $33,154.00, of which the State of Wisconsin contributed only $649.77. In that year, too, Oshkosh itself spent $16,240 on poor relief, of which clothing amounted to $174.26, fuel to $3,328.96, rent to $1,806.20 and food to $6,386.30.[22]

Relief schedules of the time reveal what provisions the poor were allowed. Every month the allowance was: 1 lb. of coffee, ¼ lb. of tea or 1 lb. of cocoa, 2 ½ lbs. of sugar, 2 lbs. of prunes or 2 cans of tomatoes, 1 lb. of rice or split peas, 1 ½ lbs. of oatmeal or 2 lbs. of corn-meal, 1 package of yeast foam, 1 small sack of salt, 1 ounce of pepper, 1 quart of vinegar, 1 lb. of macaroni and 5 gallons of kerosene. For children under the age of fourteen, each child was allowed per month: 1 pint of milk per day, 4 lbs. of oatmeal, 3 lbs. of sugar, 1 quart of Karo syrup, 8 loaves of bread, 16 lbs. of potatoes, 1 lb. of rice, 2 lbs. of boiling meat, ½ lb. of lard and one can of tomatoes. The city also provided fuel and rent and free medical attention. The physician in attendance could prescribe necessities not provided in the list above.[23] There were complaints that the poor were also being furnished with the "best of merchandise" such as pineapples, lemons, salmon, olives, grapes, pears, Fig Newtons and oysters. To end such extravagance the City Council resolved that "the City Poor Commissioner be instructed to refrain from providing the resident poor with other than staple groceries except on the written order of the city physician and that all bills be itemized when presented to the council."[24]

In addition to the State Department of Public Welfare and the money expended by the Oshkosh municipal government, contributions were also raised by the community through the auspices of the Welfare Fund which supplied monies to local agencies such as the Bureau of Family Services, the Ladies Benevolent Society, Mercy Circle (which maintained a hospital bed at Mercy Hospital), the Charity Circle, which gave care and medical attention to needy mothers, the Red Cross, the War Veterans' Bureau, the Visiting Nurses Association, the Oshkosh Girl's Club, the Campfire Girls, and the Oshkosh Council of Boy Scouts.[25]

The effect of the Crash was felt at once. On November 1, the Ford Motor Car Company took out a full-page advertisement in the *Oshkosh Northwestern* announcing an immediate reduction in the price of cars and trucks. Ford believed that "industry and business are sound. Every indication is that general business conditions will remain prosperous. We are reducing prices now because we feel that such a step is the best contribution that could be made to assure a continuation of good business throughout the country." Roadsters were reduced from $460 to $435; Town Cars from $1,400 to $1,200.[26]

The Oshkosh city government also began to curb expenditures. The Board of Education decided to abandon a visiting teacher plan which would have consisted of one teacher. The Board found that the salary of $1,800 was too burdensome "due to the unpromising aspect of business employment conditions in general."[27]

Throughout November employment for unskilled labor began to dry up. On November 22, Murt Malone, superintendent of the Oshkosh Public Employment Service, maintained, in part, by the Wisconsin Industrial Commission, sent a letter to about 350 merchants and manufacturers requesting aid in solving the unemployment situation.[28] "Each day," he wrote, "we have hundreds of worthy applicants applying to us who desire work, not charity and who are most eager to accept anything offered...". Malone went on to explain that jobs lasting only a few days or hours should be reported since they were better than nothing to those without a means of earning a living.[29]

The approaching holiday season highlighted the worsening conditions. In an attempt to alleviate some of the distress, the Oshkosh Recreation Department, as it had done in 1928, put on a show in a local cinema at which things "good to eat" were accepted in place of cash admission. This brought in 14 bushels of potatoes, 3 bushels of carrots, cabbage and apples as well as 185 kinds of canned goods, in all amounting to about $150 in value. In Menasha, the Red Cross arranged a Thanksgiving matinee at the local theater which resulted in 43 families receiving groceries valued at $125.00.[30]

The *Oshkosh Northwestern* still looked hopefully to the future. On the day before Thanksgiving it declared "the country can be thankful that in spite of the recent collapse of the stock market and the temporary slackening in some major lines of industry, business in general is sound and there is a well-defined trend for improvement. That the year 1930 will be a busy and prosperous one is the prospect." The editorial went on to praise the President for all that he was doing and ended by saying, "when it comes to business statesmanship, it is hats off to President Hoover."[31]

This optimism was echoed by many businessmen in Oshkosh who released information that their factories were still working at or near capacity and would only shut down for repairs and inventory. The situation in the Wisconsin Axle plant was very good, officials stated. All departments were operating on a full schedule of ten hours a day and a six-day week; even night shifts were necessary for several months to maintain production. At the Badger Lumber and Manufacturing Company, which made boxes, chairs and other pieces of light furniture, officials reported that the number of employees was larger "than at any time this year." At the Radford-Wright plant, which made door and window frames, the work schedule was nine hours a day, five days a week with about a 75% capacity crew. However, some plants admitted to curtailing the work force, describing it as being more or less a provisional condition. J.L. Clark, a manufacturer of auto bodies, explained that it was working at one-third capacity but this was temporary. Plant operation on a full schedule of ten hours, six days a week was anticipated by the middle of December.[32]

The year ended on a less sanguine note than the *Oshkosh Northwestern* had anticipated. In the interest of economy, for example, Neenah's city government canceled all municipal building projects except for some street paving.[33] Indeed, at this time Menasha was so short of cash that the city government resolved to borrow from a local bank $50,000 at 5 ½% in order to pay current and ordinary expenses.[34] The situation was altogether rockier elsewhere in Wisconsin. Business failures in the state for the year numbered 481 firms with total debts of $7,975,240.[35] Between October 15 and December 15 the index of aggregate factory payrolls dropped from 103.7 to 88.2.

This was the most precipitous and extensive decline on record since the Crash of 1921. From November 15 to December 15 Wisconsin's manufacturing Employment decreased 4.8 % and aggregate payrolls declined 11.6%. Oshkosh followed the trend. During 1929, of the 6,046 persons applying for work, 1,772 remained idle.[36] Moreover, in Winnebago County delinquent real estate taxes amounted to $94,248.93 of which Oshkosh's share came to $57,637.81.[37]

These signs notwithstanding, Professor C.F. Crowe, head of the Economics Department at Lawrence College in Appleton, told the Neenah Kiwanis Club that the crash was temporary and had reached the bottom. The business prospect for the United States was "very bright for 1930." Favorable indicators in Europe, he explained, would lead to American exports to Europe, especially for a farm industry that had become stabilized. Moreover, American corporations had large reserves of cash and are willing to expand their operations by investing in improvements. Furthermore, the workability of the Federal Reserve System would assure business stability."[38]

Professor Crowe's prophesy was underscored on December 30, 1929 by an editorial in Neenah's The Daily News-Times which predicted: "1930 will be a prosperous year. The country has already recovered from the uncertainty of the recent stock market recession and business leaders are planning for the future with courage and confidence."[39] It would take the dawning of a new year to see if this was mere wishful thinking.

Notes

1. The last serious financial decline had occurred in the early 1920s when the Gross National Product (GNP) slumped from $88.9 billion in 1920 to $74 billion in 1921 and 1922. Thereafter the GNP rose steadily reaching $104.4billion in 1929. At the same time per capita income went from $672 in 1922 to $857 in 1929. See George Brown Tindall, *America: A Narrative History*. (NY: W.W. Norton & Co., 1984), vol.2, p. 1035.
2. Quoted in Gilbert Burck and Charles E. Silberman, "Why the Depression Lasted So Long," *Fortune, Vol. LI, No.3 (March 1955)*, p. 89.
3. *The Daily Northwestern*, October 26, 1929. [Hereafter *Oshkosh Northwestern*]. This paper enjoyed the largest circulation throughout Winnebago County. It leaned heavily toward conservative Republican politics in its editorial opinions.
4. U.S. Department of Commerce, *National Income: A Supplement to the Survey of Current Business*, 1951 ed. (Washington, 1951), pp. 158-59, as quoted in *Hitting Home: The Great Depression in Town and Country*, edited by Bernard Sternsher (Chicago: Quadrangle Books, 1970), p. 164; U.S. Bureau of the Census, *Historical Statistics of the United States: Colonial Times to 1957*, as quoted in Paul W. Glad, *War, A New Era, and Depression, 1914-1940 [The History of Wisconsin, Vol.5]* (Madison: State Historical Society of Wisconsin, 1990), p. 356.
5. *Oshkosh Northwestern*, October 29, 1929.
6. Sternsher, *The Great Depression in Town and Country*, p. 164.
7. Glad, *War, A New Era, and Depression*, p. 348.
8. *Oshkosh Northwestern*, February 22, 1930.
9. State Historical Society of Wisconsin/Archives [Hereafter SHSW/Archives], Industrial Commission of Wisconsin. Wisconsin State Employment Service Library Reports, 1920-43, Series No. 1026, Box No.1, "Effects of the Economic Depression on Employment and Earnings, Bankruptcies and Bank Failures, and the Cost of Public Relief in Wisconsin."
10. The Sixteenth National Business Conference at Wellesley, *Commercial and Financial Chronicle*, September 21, 1929, p. 1800, as quoted in Harris G. Warren, *Herbert Hoover and the Great Depression* (NY: Oxford University Press), p. 103.
11. As quoted in Judith S. Baughman, *American Decade, 1920-1929* (NY: Gale Research Inc., 1996), p. 102.
12. *The Daily News-Times* [Neenah], September 23, 1929. This optimistic assertion was challenged by the fact that in Wisconsin there was an increase of 16% in the value of manufactured products and of 32% in the value added by manufacturing in the decade of the 1920s. This increase occurred in spite of a decline of 25% in the general level of wholesale price of non-agricultural commodities, so that it reflected a much greater increase in the quantity of manufactured goods produced. Despite this great increase in production, however, the number of manufacturing establishments in Wisconsin decreased by 39% and the number of persons engaged in manufacturing by 1%. The average number of wage earners employed in Wisconsin factories in 1929 was only a few hundred more than the number employed in 1919. The decrease in the number of establishments was much greater in Wisconsin than in the country as a whole, but in the value of manufactured products and in the value added by manufacture Wisconsin had a somewhat greater increase than the entire United States. The average number of wage earners employed in manufacturing decreased throughout the country by nearly 2% while it increased slightly in Wisconsin. See Wisconsin Blue Book 1933, p. 125. [Hereafter WBB].

13. *Fifteenth U.S. Census*, 1930, Vol. 3, Part 2, p. 1319. Wisconsin in 1930 was the 13th state in population in the U.S.A., a rank which it held in the previous three censuses. Total population in 1930 was 2,939,000 as compared with 2,632,067 in 1920. The increase in population was very unevenly distributed throughout the state. More than 60$ of the total increase was accounted for by Milwaukee county alone and most of the rest of a half-dozen other counties. Wisconsin in 1930 was by no means densely populated. In 1930 it had a population equal to only 58 people per square mile. This, however, was higher than any state west of the Mississippi River. The census of 1930 was the most extensive ever undertaken in the U.S. To the reports on population, agriculture, manufactures, and mining were added, in 1930, a census of distribution and construction industries and of unemployment. *WBB 1930*, pp. 103-04.
14. Peace Lutheran Church, *Confirmation and Marriages Book*, 1928-1975.
15. *Basic Facts of Oshkosh, Wis.*, (Oshkosh: City Planning Commission, 1951), p. 2. Also see *Fifteenth U.S. Census, 1930, Vol. 3, Part 2, p. 1344.*
16. University of Wisconsin-Oshkosh Area Research Center [hereafter OWO-ARC) Winnebago Series 82, City of Menasha. Resolutions of the Common Council 1927-1933, Box 3, Folder 4, No. 271.
17. UWO-ARC, Folder 3, Resolution No. 247, June 18, 1929.
18. *Menasha Record* [hereafter *MR*], March 5, 1931.
19. *Fifteenth U.S. Census*, 1930, Vol. 3, Part 2, p. 1344. In 1930, Wisconsin was the tenth state in manufactures--a rank which it held since 1900. Approximately 25% more of its people were engaged in manufacturing than in agriculture, and the value added by manufacture was considerably more than twice as great as the gross value of all farm production. Yet Wisconsin had only a little more than 3% of the total manufactures of the United States, WBB 1933, p. 123.
20. SHSW/Archives. Department of Public Relief. Division of Public Assistance. Unemployment Relief Administrative Records, 1931-1933. Series No. 1410. Box No. 2, Folder: 1932 Estimated Poor Relief, "Poor Relief Expenditures within Counties of Wisconsin, 1928-1932" and also Box No. 4, Folder: Relief Oshkosh, "Distribution of Funds 1928, Overseer of Poor." See as well Box No. 4, Folder: Relief Mothers' Pension, Tabulation of Amount of Money Expended under the Aid to Dependent Children's Law.
21. *Oshkosh Northwestern*, November 22, 1929.
22. SHSW/Archives, Department of Public Relief, Division of Public Assistance. Unemployment Relief Administrative Records, 1931-1933. Series No. 1410. Box No. 4, Folder: Relief/Oshkosh, "Distribution of Funds 1928, Overseer of Poor."
23. *Oshkosh Northwestern*, February 18, 1927, p. 12.
24. *Oshkosh Northwestern*, January 18, 1927.
25. *Oshkosh Northwestern*, October 24, 1929.
26. *Oshkosh Northwestern*, November 21, 1929.
27. *Oshkosh Northwestern*, November 2, 1929.
28. The Wisconsin Industrial Commission was the labor department of the state. A special department to enforce state labor law, the Bureau of Labor Statistics, had been created in 1887. In 1911, when the Workmen's Compensation Law was enacted, this was replaced by the Industrial Commission which consisted of three commissioners appointed by the governor, subject to confirmation by the senate, for six-year terms. The Commission was divided into a number of departments which included Safety & Sanitation (the largest), Women & Child Labor, Statistics, Employment & Unemployment Relief. The last of these departments maintained nine offices throughout Wisconsin. Oshkosh was

one of these. The offices were conducted under a cooperative arrangement with the city (or city and county combined) in which they were located whereby the Commission paid the salaries of employees and the local community paid all other expenses. There was no charge made for the services rendered by these employment offices, which in normal times found jobs for more than 100,000 persons each year. WBB, pp. 33-35.
29. *Oshkosh Northwestern*. November 22, 1929.
30. *Oshkosh Northwestern*, November 27, 1929; *MR*, December 11, 1929.
31. *Oshkosh Northwestern*, November 27, 1929.
32. *Oshkosh Northwestern*, November 27, 1929. In its budget for 1930, the Menasha Common Council, in a clear sign that hard times had not yet made an appearance, set aside only $3,200 for poor relief as opposed to $4,000 for snow and ice removal. See UWO-ARC. Winnebago Series 82, City of Menasha. City Clerk. Resolutions of the Common Council, 1870-1964. Box 3, Folder 4, Resolutions of the Common Council, 1927-1933, Resolution No. 259, December 3, 1929.
33. The Daily News-Times, December 3, 1929.
34. UWO-ARC. Winnebago Series No. 82. City of Menasha. City Clerk. Resolutions of the Common Council, 1927-1933, Folder 3, No. 247, October 2, 1929.
35. *Oshkosh Northwestern*, February 22, 1930.
36. Wisconsin Labor Market Report [hereafter WLMR), January 30, 1930, vol. 10, no. 1, pp. 1, 17.
37. *MR*, March 25, 1931.
38. *The Daily News-Times*, December 12, 1929, and *MR*, December 12, 1929.
39. *The Daily News-Times*, December 30, 1929.

Chapter 2

1930: The Onset of Depression

The situation in early 1930 was not encouraging. In February, the Bureau of Family Service declared that unemployment in the previous three months was the chief reason 216 families comprising 957 people appealed to the Bureau for aid.[1] Organized in 1907 as the Associated Charities, the Bureau of Family Service was incorporated in 1921. As well as dispensing financial aid, its purpose was "to assist individuals and families in difficulty to develop the capacity for solving their own problems." This was carried out "through social casework, education for better family living and participation in community welfare planning."[2] As there was no Juvenile Protective Association or Association for the Prevention of Juvenile Delinquency, the Bureau also acted in such capacity as far as possible.[3]

By now not only ordinary laborers were in distress, the Crash was beginning to affect businesses as well. In March, the officers of the Menasha Wood Split Pulley Company wrote Mayor W.E. Held, requesting a delay of three to four months in the payment of the company's personal property taxes due to "general business conditions."[4] Three months later, the Wisconsin Container Corporation went even further when it petitioned the city government for a refund of personal property and real estate taxes for five years. The city agreed, realizing the great economic value of the company.[5]

Hard times notwithstanding, the mayor and members of the city council of Oshkosh were quick to take advantage of an increase in the size of the city to raise their salaries. According to the law, the salaries of city heads were to be $5,000 and $4,500 minimum when the local population reached the 40,000 mark. In the census of 1930, it was revealed that the population of Oshkosh had increased from 33,162 in 1920 to 40,108 in 1930. This permitted an increase in the mayor's salary from $4,000 to $5,000 a year and that of council members from $3,500 to $4,500.[6]

Despite marked declines in economic activity, there was still some expression of optimism. An editorial in the *Oshkosh Northwestern* quoted President Hoover's contention that all evidence indicated "the worst effects of the stock market crash upon employment will have passed during the next sixty days with the amelioration of seasonal employment, the gaining strength of other forces, and the continued co-operation of the many agencies actively cooperating with the government to restore business and relieve distress."[7] The editorial was wrong. Hoover was wrong. The situation was to get much worse.

In order to restore a positive economic climate, Hoover wanted a partnership between business and labor that would counteract the economic disaster. In late winter/early spring 1930, therefore, Hoover called the nation's economic leaders into conference and secured pledges to maintain wages and minimize layoffs, expand construction, and avoid strikes and lockouts. Moreover, he persuaded the United States Chamber of Commerce to set up organizations through which its constituent trade associations could work for the implementation of these pledges, while also calling for government credit, spending and tax policies that would support and supplement these business undertakings.[8] Speaking once again to the Chamber of Commerce on May 1, Hoover asserted that employment was rising and would continue to do so, that the great associations representative of American economic life had demonstrated their capacity to mobilize individual initiative in times of stress and that the experience had succeeded to a remarkable degree and should be studied "with a view to broad determination of what can be done to achieve greater stability for the future."[9]

In Wisconsin by this time, Governor Walter Kohler had begun to realize that the Depression was shaking his popularity and that of the Republican Party. Like Hoover, he, too, wanted to see a partnership develop between business and labor that would overcome economic difficulties. Similarly, he was against broad action by government (federal or state) to restore prosperity, fearing that such action might lead to inappropriate interference in the activities of business. For a time at least, he followed Hoover's policy of minimizing the seriousness of the crisis, although Kohler never went so far as Hoover when the president remarked that as a cure for the Depression "what the country needs is a good big laugh."[10] That government should stay out of the economy was a notion on the wane in Wisconsin by the summer of 1930. Kohler realized this and as a first, modest step established a Citizens' Committee on Unemployment to study the crisis and make recommendations concerning ways of dealing with it. To head the committee, he appointed Don Lescohier, professor of labor economics at the University of Wisconsin.

By this time other business leaders were coming around to the same point of view. In Winnebago County, Frank Bateman Keefe, vice-president and director of the Oshkosh Building & Loan Association, in a strident speech, also pressed for government to provide work:

> It is nothing short of criminal that honest men and women in the richest country on earth should be required to walk the streets for months, begging and pleading for a chance to work...I am one who believes that the time for engaging people in public construction work is dur-

ing periods such as this of industrial depression. If courthouses or other public buildings are to be erected they should be constructed during such times as this in order to relieve in a measure the unemployment situation. Roads should be built and all public works pushed to absorb as much as possible the unemployment problem.[11]

September was primary month. As the Democratic Party was all but moribund, all action centered around the two wings of the Republican Party, the Stalwarts and the Progressives. Philip La Follette, the son of the former governor and dynamo, Robert La Follette, represented the Progressives and undertook a spirited campaign. He spent little time talking about the Depression itself. Rather, he attacked big business which he asserted was in league with the Stalwarts, an alliance that would lead to the loss of control over the government by ordinary citizens. Kohler, believing himself secure in the affection of the voters, campaigned rather casually. The primary held on September 16, 1930 was a shock for the Stalwarts. La Follette won handily, presaging an assured victory in the general election in November when, probably, he would face weak opposition from the Democratic candidate, Charles Hemmersley.

As the summer waned, economic conditions in Winnebago County grew steadily worse. The average per capita weekly earnings of factory workers in Oshkosh over the year had declined 10.8% from $20.05 in September 1929 to $17.88 in September 1930. In Neenah and Menasha, despite growing unemployment, the decline of 3.4% was not nearly so marked ($23.10 to $21.31).[12]

By early October, the economy continued to slump throughout the state and the Wisconsin Citizens' Committee on Unemployment sent a letter to all the chairmen of county boards of supervisors:

> We are approaching a hard winter. Distress and suffering will be more general and severe than last winter. Many who have never before asked for help have been out of work for months. Some have not been able to get work for an entire year. Having now exhausted their savings and credit they are forced to ask for aid.

The committee then urged the supervisors to double or more than double their usual budgets for poor relief. It found that in many communities three times as many families as usual had asked for relief during the past summer. It believed that this number would "undoubtedly increase during the coming winter months." It was "unquestionably" the duty of the tax-supported agencies to see that the citizens of their communities were to be provided with the necessities of life. Moreover, county boards should be prepared to assist those temporarily unemployed in order that families would not lose their homes or lack necessary medical attention and children be forced to drop out of school. The committee also pointed out that in many counties money had been spent in a haphazard and unsystematic way. When only a few thousand dollars were allocated to a few needy families it was not a serious problem, the committee declared, but when the budget and needs increased it became important that the work be handled in a centralized and systematic way by trained persons.[13]

At the end of October, the Citizens' Committee made public its recommendations. It urged equalizing unemployment among families where too many in one family worked in one place. The committee wished to eliminate some of these workers and give their jobs to the heads of other families. It also wanted to discontinue overtime and thereby employ more people. In addition, it hoped to maintain wage scales because reductions accentuated the Depression by decreasing purchasing power. Finally, it urged that all repair work be done at once as prices were as low as they could possibly fall and consumers who had been holding back on purchases would help relieve the situation through "moral buying."[14]

Although laudable, the Committee's recommendations did not provide tangible solutions for the problems presented in 1930. By contrast, a practical plan was advanced by the city government of Oshkosh which decided it would use men with families to support rather than machines on an excavation for a new sewer on Waugoo Street. Thirty men, to be paid 40 to 50 cents an hour, were to do the digging; this would involve from fourteen to eighteen more men than if machines were to be used. It was reckoned that the work would last from two weeks to a month and cost no more than $1,500.[15]

This attempt at Luddism[16] provoked criticism. John R. Commons, a nationally known professor of labor economics at the University of Wisconsin, argued: "The Oshkosh idea would be unsound as public policy. If we were to discard machinery that would increase labor costs to the taxpayers and the taxpayers would not stand for it very long. It is not justifiable to increase taxes wastefully. Relieving unemployment by that method would amount to a dole system."[17]

A counter-argument was quick in coming. "They're crazy," Councilman Henry Hagene retorted. "We're not opposed to the use of machinery. We are recommending man-labor as an emergency relief proposition, and only for this one project. We're trying to help the working people."[18]

At the same time another councilman, George F. Oaks, suggested a plan which he dubbed, "Loan Your Job a Week," under which portions of all city crews would be laid off for weekly intervals to give work to men with families who had been unemployed for long periods of time. "Those men," Oaks claimed, "who had been steadily employed by the city...should consider it a patriotic duty to sacrifice a portion of their pay...to aid restoration of better conditions throughout the city." The plan of alternating crews would practically double the number of men then on the city payroll. In each of the city departments, where possible, Oaks explained, "some men will be asked to take a short lay-off, say a week or so in order that some unfortunate father of a family will at least have a chance to earn and reestablish his credit." Oaks continued, "I am

The Onset of Depression

sure, that it will not be asking too much. I have seen, able-bodied men, with responsibilities that married life brings in absolute want, not asking for charity, or for the opinion of some expert on economics as to the condition of business, but for an opportunity to earn enough to supply their families with the necessities of life...". Loan Your Job a Week received approval of the various city foremen and superintendents. Oaks then announced that it would go into effect at once and would give employment to about thirty men a week and would be continued until harsh winter weather halted all outdoor city work. The day after the plan was revealed in the newspaper, 300 men flocked to the city hall to apply for the thirty jobs. The program evoked limited enthusiasm among the unemployed and lasted only a fortnight. During that time ninety-six men were given temporary employment at an average wage of 44 ½ cents per hour.[19]

When inspiration failed to stimulate the economy, imagination assumed its moment in Oshkosh's attempt to deal with the widespread unemployment. The H.P. Schmidt Milling Company took on men and women to walk door-to door to promote the company's new "Honey Dew Flour." Homemakers were challenged to bake their own bread, save money, and provide work for the sales force. The company enjoyed some initial success, but it was limited and hardly addressed the growing unemployment dilemma.[20]

A more concerted effort was then undertaken by the local American Legion post as part of a national scheme to assault unemployment. Late in 1931, Herbert Hoover, still reluctant to abandon his "voluntarism" approach to the economic crisis, called upon the American Legion to post sponsor drives to assist the unemployed. Hundreds volunteered to provide projects and labor to sustain the effort. It was all very solemn. A local Oshkosh priest, Father William A. Reul, gave the invocation which cast the Legion's plan in the same light as the crusades against the infidel during the Middle Ages. The proceedings included a public pledge "to support and devote my best efforts...to the end that I may help my fellow citizens and thereby hasten the return of prosperity." It was reported that over three-hundred citizen took the pledge at the first public meeting held in February 1932. The entire staff at the First National Bank pledged to provide 751 hours of labor, translated into 18 weeks of work per person.[21]

Carlton Foster, general chairman of the Committee on Civic Unemployment, revealed that experts had examined the economy and had determined that the building sector was the one area ripe for a revival. To wit, captains were appointed for each city ward with the charge of conducting an extensive inventory of homes which could use remodeling. Local construction companies and mill owners were expected to provide building materials at cut-rate prices and homeowners were encouraged that this was the time to "Re-Roof, Repair, Re-Build and Re-Paint." Even renters and homeowners with no work to be performed could purchase labor certificates. Men would be hired at 35 cents an hour and women at 25 cents to do whatever the purchaser might want done. The American Legion, a collaborator in this scheme, hoped that Oshkosh would accrue benefits to the same degree as Muncie, Indiana, a city comparable in size, which had pumped more than $300,000 into the local economy. Despite the generous endorsement, the Legion plan, like other schemes during this era, failed to fundamentally alter the desperate state of the economy or local unemployment.[22]

Another problem that troubled the city fathers in Winnebago County was the transient unemployed. *The Daily News-Times* of Neenah editorialized about the matter. Although hoboes were put up in the Neenah jail normally, it was now becoming overcrowded. The editorial allowed that these transients were not ordinarily hoboes but men who wanted jobs. However, the city, it warned, ought not to provide facilities better than the jail as that would encourage vagrants to come to Neenah to stay for more than just a night or two.[23] After a cursory investigation of the problem, the Neenah city council discovered that on average over twenty homeless men were given lodging in the jail each night, far exceeding its capacity and creating an unsatisfactory condition. Hence the Committee on Police and Health was directed to seek a suitable place in the basement of the city hall to provide a night's lodging, always under police supervision, for the men.[24]

Effie R. Bishop, Neenah's poor commissioner, reported at this time to the city council about a problem that troubled her. She was besieged with requests, rather demands, for aid from indigent families who drifted to Neenah from other cities. "Those who come are reluctant to leave, most having the impression that Neenah feeds its indigents well," she proclaimed. To make her point, Bishop cited the example of a large family from Milwaukee who "inflicted" themselves on Neenah and "loudly demanded aid." Milwaukee authorities advised the poor commissioner and they would "care for the family if it is sent back there but will not feed it here." Although the Neenah poor department bought tickets to transport the family to Milwaukee, they refused to leave and insisted upon being supported in Neenah. Bishop made persuasive effort to get them to leave and the family finally departed for Milwaukee. But in this conjunction, the poor commissioner underscored the fact, should the city council have missed it, that help for families drifting into Neenah depleted limited funds that should be used for local families who are suffering very real hardship and deprivation "directly due to the present economic conditions." But the anomaly of anomalies, some families were too proud to accept aid even when it was offered because, Bishop observed, they did not want their names published (as was usually done) in the newspapers or on posters in city hall. At Bishop's urging, the city council passed a motion to desist from this practice so that "those who really needed aid badly and were deserving of it would apply for help."[25] By the end of December, twenty-nine families had applied and the poor commissioner's report for that month showed a total of $1,019.80 spent on relief work.[26]

Meanwhile, the regular election was held. Hemmersley campaigned with vigor, denouncing his opponents for the Depression. "Republicans are responsi-

The Onset of Depression

ble for hard times," he insisted. A Democratic administration, he explained, "would have prevented the panic of 1929 because it would not have fostered and abetted the saturnalia of stock jobbing on Wall Street. There is no question that the orgy of speculation carried on in 1928 and 1929 had the support and encouragement of the administration in Washington..."[27] Nevertheless, La Follette with 392,958 votes won easily over Hemmersley (170,020). In Republican Winnebago County, however, Hemmersley did not do badly, receiving 7,116 votes, quite close to La Follette's 7,555.[28] All Winnebago County representatives in the State House, everyone of them a Republican were re-elected.[29] In the nation as a whole, however, the Democrats did very well, obtaining their first national victory since 1916. They now held a majority in the House and made enough of a showing in the Senate to control it in coalition with western agrarians.[30]

At about the same time as the elections, the Winnebago County Board of Supervisors held its annual November meeting. The unemployment issue was discussed. One problem to be faced was that pointed out by Lescohier of the Citizens' Committee on Unemployment in his October 4 letter to county boards of supervisors concerning the decentralization of poor relief which was causing needless expense in administering the law. For remedy, the Board decided that from January 1, 1931 all poor relief in the county would be unified in one department of outdoor relief and, hence, the expense of maintaining poor persons within the county was to be a county charge. Furthermore, it created an office of overseer of the poor. No action was taken, however, because Frank B. Keefe, the county district attorney, told the board that legal problems concerning centralization would have to be settled first, with the result that nothing was done for two years.[31]

A report of the Board's committee on unemployment followed at another session. The committee explained that it was unable to obtain complete statistics on jobless people in the county. From the federal employment office, however, the committee had learned that of the 100 or so applicants for male help the office received on an average day, only nine could be placed in some kind of job. Local factories, operating at about 50% of capacity, were working their men in shifts so that they could receive at least some pay. What was to be done? The law did not permit the county board to hand over money as a dole to the unemployed. One thing it could do, however, was to allocate money to provide work on county improvements. In consequence, the committee made a number of suggestions: first, to appoint another committee to discover how many men or families were out of work; second, to raise $100,000 in tax revenues for a contingent fund to help unemployment in specified projects: a) place at the disposal of the highway committee as many men as it could reasonably use in road building, snow removal and the like; b) develop a city park in Oshkosh and construct a new county court house. It was all a moot point; the $100,000 was a sticking point and the Board rejected it.[32]

What the Board faced was a reflection of what was going on in the rest of Wisconsin. By December 1930, twenty-four banks had been suspended and 656 businesses had failed in the state. There were now in the state 23.6% fewer employees on factory payrolls than in April 1929. Corresponding payrolls had decreased 40.2%. Since December 1929 factory employment had declined 21.5% while corresponding payrolls dipped 27.6%. During 1930, moreover, the nine public employment offices had found jobs for only $52,021 persons in contrast with 101,183 in 1929. Overall the cost of outdoor relief in Wisconsin for 1930 amounted to $2,400,000, double that of 1928 which was considered a normal year. The amount did not include institutional relief, mothers' aid, pensions for soldiers' and sailors' relief, moreover, these figures did not list relief given by private agencies, churches, lodges, and so forth.[33] Poor relief expenditures in 1930 for Winnebago County came to $134,202 as opposed to $104,243 in 1928. These figures quickly expressed themselves in the growth of local poor relief. In Neenah, for example, relief rose from $2,853.39 in 1928 to $5,047.86 in 1930. In Menasha, the numbers grew from $2,713.18 (1928) to $5,036.91 (1930).[34]

Everyone agreed that 1930 had been dreadful and all were looking forward to 1931 as a year of hope. The business magazine, *Forbes*, spoke for many when it declared:

> Goodbye 1930! Though the chastening may have been salutary, we bid thee farewell without regret. We feel we have had enough of depression and disappointment, deflation and despair, losses and lost jobs. We gladly turn over the leaf in the Book of Time. Welcome 1931! We christen thee Recovery Year.[35]

The *Oshkosh Northwestern*, for its part, waxed lyrical over what was to happen in 1931. "Captains of big industries," it intoned, "are already planning for full speed ahead. Sound judgment and decisive planning and execution can quickly dispel the remainder of the gloom and set the sun of prosperity to shining brightly."[36] While waiting for the gloom to dissipate, however, the Oshkosh city government prudently distributed from the municipal warehouse 800 pounds of free, fresh fish to the public.[37] A few days later, William A. Meyer of Oshkosh, introduced into the Wisconsin Assembly a bill to permit ice fishing on all lakes and streams in the state which he said would benefit many families who were financially strapped and found it "difficult to replenish the household larder from other sources."[38]

Notes

1. *Oshkosh Northwestern*, February 14, 1930.
2. Clinton Karstaedt, ed., *Oshkosh: One Hundred Years a City, 1853-1953.* (Oshkosh, 1953), pp. 29-30.
3. *Oshkosh Northwestern*, November 2, 1932.

The Onset of Depression

4. UWO-ARC. Winnebago Series 84. City of Menasha. City Clerk's Papers, 1855-1964. Box 1, Folder 29, City Budget and Taxes, 1929-1930.
5. UWO-ARC. Winnebago Series 82. City of Menasha. City Clerk, Resolutions of the Common Council, 1870-1964. Box 3, Folder 4, Resolutions of the Common Council, 1927-1933, Resolution No. 302, June 17, 1930.
6. *Oshkosh Northwestern*, January 16, 1931.
7. *Oshkosh Northwestern*, March 10, 1930.
8. Robert Lamont, "The White House Conferences," *Journal of Business*, No. 3 (July 1930), pp. 269-71.
9. Office of the Federal Register, *Public Papers of the Presidents of the United States: Herbert Hoover, 1930.* (Washington: Government Printing Office, 1976), pp. 78-83; 171-79.
10. John C. Challberg, et. al. *The Great Depression: Opposing Viewpoints.* (San Diego: Greenhaven Press, 1994), p. 14.
11. UWO-ARCH Osh, Mss., BW, Frank Bateman Keefe Papers, 1930-1975, Box 1, Folder 6, *Address at the Unveiling of a Marker for the First House Built in Oshkosh, June 14, 1930.* Keefe served as district attorney for Winnebago County from 1922 to 1928. In November 1930 he was re-elected to this post. Beginning in 1938, as part of the Republican resurgence in Wisconsin, he was elected to Congress where he served six terms.
12. *WLMR*, Vol. 10, No. 9, September 1930, p. 9.
13. SHSW Archives. Department of Public Welfare. Division of Public Assistance. Unemployment Relief Administration Records, 1921-1933. Series No. 1410, Box No. 2, Folder: Relief Committee--General Folder 1930-1931, Letter of October 4, 1930 by Don Lescohier, Wisconsin Citizens' Committee on Unemployment to Chairmen of County Boards of Supervisors.
14. *Oshkosh Northwestern*, October 29, 1930.
15. *Oshkosh Northwestern*, October 28, 1930.
16. Luddism occurred in Britain between 1811 and 1816 when textile workers sabotaged and destroyed machinery which they believed was taking away their jobs.
17. *Oshkosh Northwestern*, October 30, 1930.
18. *Oshkosh Northwestern*, October 30, 1930. Another recommendation was made by the Wisconsin Executive Council of the American Legion which proposed that men out of work be allowed in the Army Reserve for the duration of the Depression. The plan would permit any unemployed man to enlist and draw regular army pay. It would be necessary to change the age limit, however, so that middle-aged and married men could be accepted. The enlistee would remain in the Reserve until he procured a job. The Council offered the plan as a substitute for a dole system which it did not favor. See *Oshkosh Northwestern*, October 27, 1930.
19. *Oshkosh Northwestern*, November 1, 1930; November 3, 1930. Also see George F. Oaks, "Oshkosh Helps Unemployment Situation," in *The Municipality*. Vol. 26 (January 1931), p. 2. See also Oaks, "Oshkosh Helps Unemployment Situation," p. 12.
20. Michael Goc, *Oshkosh 150 Years, p. 57.*
21. *Oshkosh Northwestern*, February 22, 1932.
22. *Oshkosh Northwestern*, February 22, 1932. The Legion spelled out its plan with a two-page advertisement in the *Oshkosh Northwestern* with the glowing banner headline:

"Here is the Employment Plan That Can Bring Back Prosperity to Oshkosh." See *Oshkosh Northwestern, February 22, 1932.*
23. *Daily News-Times,* October 10, 1930.
24. *MR,* November 6, 1930. According to Chief of Police James Lyman's report there were 986 transients in 1930. See Unemployment Relief Administration Records, Series No. 1410, Box No. 3, Folder: Relief Menasha (Winnebago 6), newspaper clipping, probably *Appleton Post Crescent,* January 1932.
25. *MR,* December 8, 1930.
26. *MR,* January 8, 1931.
27. *Oshkosh Northwestern,* October 29, 1930.
28. *WBB,* 1931, p. 4.
29. *Oshkosh Northwestern,* January 5, 1931.
30. Tindall, *America: A Narrative History,* vol.2, p. 1054.
31. The report of this meeting was published in the *Oshkosh Northwestern,* January 17, 1931. See a revisit to this issue in *MR,* March 4, 1932.
32. *MR,* January 17, 1931.
33. *WLMR,* Vol. 11, January 1931, No. 1, p. 1 and Vol.13, January 1933, No. 1, p. 28. *Effects of the Economic Depression on Employment and Earnings, Bankruptcies, and Bank Failures, and the Cost of Public Relief in Wisconsin. Industrial Commission of Wisconsin, Miscellaneous Reports, 1920-1963,* p. 34. Harris Gaylord Warren, *Herbert Hoover and the Great Depression* (NY: Oxford University Press, 1959), p. 132. Also see Unemployed Relief Administration Records, 1931-1933, Series No. 1410, Box No. 2, Folder: 1932 Estimated Poor Relief, Memorandum of Poor Relief Expenditures within Counties of Wisconsin, 1928-1932. Refer to Lester V. Chandler, *America's Greatest Depression, 1929-1941* NNY: Harper & Row Publishers, 1970), p. 5.
34. SHSW-Archives, Department of Public Welfare, Division of Public Assistance. Unemployment Relief Administration Records, 1931-1933, Series 1410, Box No. 3, Folder: Relief Neenah (Winnebago 6), Memorandum of August 20, 1931 Poor Relief, Neenah, Wis. Also, Folder: Relief Menasha (Winnebago 6), Memorandum of August 21, 1931, Poor Relief Menasha, Wis.
35. As quoted in the *Oshkosh Northwestern,* January 2, 1931.
36. *Oshkosh Northwestern, January 2, 1931.*
37. *Oshkosh Northwestern,* January 2, 1931. At the same time, the City Clerk of Menasha, John Jedwabny, wrote to Senator Robert La Follette, Jr. about the problem of the workless. Most plants in town, he explained were on a part-time basis, and the poor relief appropriation had doubled; but the greatest problem, he thought, was that of the "roaming population." Federal aid, Jedwabny averred, would "assist very much." See *Oshkosh Northwestern,* January 2, 1931. He did not under-estimate the problem of the transients, of whom, according to Chief of Police James Lyman's report there were 986 in 1930. Unemployment Relief Administration Records, Series 1410, Box. No. 3, Folder: Relief Menasha (Winnebago 6), newspaper clipping, probably *Appleton Post Crescent,* January 1932.
38. *MR,* January 16, 1931.

Chapter 3

1931: The Depression Deepens

At noon on January 5, 1931, Philip La Follette, 33, took office as governor of Wisconsin. Inauguration of the youthful La Follette marked restoration of the Progressives' control in Wisconsin politics. The governor's first official act was an indication that his would be a young mens' administration. He appointed two secretaries and an executive counsel, all three under thirty years of age. La Follette recognized the proverbial "elephant in the room;" the overwhelming problem was the Depression. He strongly believed in using executive action--planning, public works, and aid for the distressed--to solve it.

Despite great hopes for 1931 and the vigorous new regime in Madison, the figures for the early months were far from reassuring. In January, the Oshkosh city budget for the year was published. The amount set aside for poor relief had now risen to $19,000, of which $10,200 was allocated for provisions, $3,200 for fuel and light, and $2,320 for rents.[1]

In early February, steps were taken to form a local body in Neenah to study the unemployment situation. A score of business and industrial leaders met in city hall in response to Major George Sande's call for cooperation with the Wisconsin Citizens' Committee on Unemployment. The chair was Henry Jung of the Hardwood Products Corporation. The group favored the establishment of an employment committee so that it could provide an exchange of ideas and statistics not only for Neenah but for other communities in the county.[2]

To give the committee some guidance, *The Menasha Record* of February 13 published an appeal by Arthur Woods, chairman of the federal emergency committee for employment. "Do not think of unemployment in terms of millions of people out of work in this broad land of America," he suggested. "Think of unemployment as a few people out of work within a stone's throw of you-- *your own neighbors*. Maybe one, or maybe two of every twenty in your vicinity." The solution, he believed, was to give a neighbor a job. To that end he listed 100 possibilities. For example, No. 10 build cupboards; No. 27, repair locks; No. 36, repair shades; No. 45, paint houses; No. 81, wash clothes; No. 82, iron clothes; No. 90, clean shoes daily; No. 92, run errands; No. 95 darn stockings; and No.

98, wash dishes. "Do this," Wood asserted, "and you are doing as patriotic a thing as any man can do. You are doing a constructive thing, a profitable thing, and a friendly thing."[3]

The Menasha Record's hortatory effort to help solve unemployment was of little consequence. Mayor N.G. Remmel of Menasha pointed out in a speech on April 20 to newly elected members of the city council that there was "an increasing demand for assistance from men and women out of work" and that included more and more unemployed homeowners. He added that the poor committee "has had a gigantic piece of work on its hands, as was indicated by the report which showed expenditures for poor relief of approximately $1,100 in March." He added that the council had "figured that $5,000 would carry us through in the poor fund but there appears to be no let up, and that amount is almost gone." The mayor went on to describe how "men and women come to us with tears in their eyes...many of them are able-bodied and because they are out of work is no fault of their own."[4]

In Oshkosh, A.M. Bleyer, director of the Oshkosh Vocational School, chipped in with his advice to handle the economic distress. In early April, he announced that courses would be offered to the unemployed during idle hours. Doubting that there would be much demand in the woodworking plants of Oshkosh in the future, coupled with the advancement of mechanization in factories, Bleyer opined that vocational schools could serve as a useful vehicle for retooling employees with "new skills for a new age." He noted that there were already twelve people coming in every day for "special training" during the month of March.[5]

Despite the great hopes for 1931 that emanated from the new regime in Madison, the figures for the early months were far from reassuring and seemed only to indicate that the depression was deepening. In January factory workers in Wisconsin had the lowest average per capita weekly earnings since January 1922. Already earnings stood at $19.70 as compared to $25.45 in January 1929 and $24.10 in January 1930. It was also estimated that there were 69,526 fewer employees on factory payrolls in Wisconsin that month than in August 1929.[6]

The difficulty in dealing with the unemployment crisis was strikingly set out by Florence Peterson, assistant secretary of the Wisconsin Citizens' Committee on Unemployment, who visited Oshkosh for several days in May 1931.[7] In her report, she began by descrying the incompetence of the former poor law commissioner (Mr. Johns) whose records she found incomplete and incoherent. She discovered that poor relief in Oshkosh had declined from $16,240 in 1928 to $14,623 in 1929 to $13,363 in 1930, a remarkable trend given the fact that it was in inverse proportion to the escalation of those in need of assistance. This occurred because the poor law commissioner had been referring unnecessarily cases to the Bureau of Family Service.[8] "Until the year 1929," she asserted, "he kept practically no books other than to list the amounts of money spent." Peterson was non-plussed by Johns' claim that since there was no need for so much unnecessary work, he made no investigations into the number of families or the individuals who were receiving assistance. Peterson was both delighted and re-

The Depression Deepens

lieved, however, to learn that an acquaintance, Frank Janda, a member of her own committee, and an Oshkosh resident, had been appointed to supersede Johns shortly before her arrival. Based on what she saw and heard, it seemed that Janda was "taking hold of the job in fine shape."[9]

But Janda, a novice in professional social work, was finding the duties of the office full of complications. The increase in the case load was becoming so heavy that he could not carry on as thorough an examination as he desired. Janda thought that a family of five could be well taken care of at the rate of $4 a week, exclusive of rent and fuel. In the matter of rent, he thought the $12 a month he allocated was too small but believed that if kept at this level it would bring down rentals even though he occasionally sanctioned payments between $15 and $18. He also paid interest on mortgages in some cases, calling it rent, to prevent families from losing homes due to foreclosure. As for food and clothing, Janda gave vouchers to applicants for purchases from "independent dealers" but not from chain stores. Considered by Peterson to be a "radical labor man," Janda discriminated against chain retailers which led one of their ranks to term him a "blankety blank."[10]

As the county's outdoor relief had not yet been centralized, Peterson found Oshkosh and other districts were still handling their own relief matters. "Each township," she explained, "looks after its own poor cases and the nature of relief varies from niggardliness to reckless extravagance, depending upon the generous nature of the commissioner, his number of friends, lodge brothers or relatives or his political ambitions." The poor commissioner's office was not the only agency in Oshkosh to provide relief. Almost as important was the Bureau of Family Service and its unofficial "specialized branches," the Mercy Circle and the Charity Circle. The Bureau paid for clothing, food, fun and some miscellaneous items. It did not pay for gas, light, water or rent. In the late 1920s the administrative costs of the Bureau, as opposed to its relief payments, were extraordinarily high. In 1928, for instance, it had expended a total of $7,228.60, of which a whopping $4,390.15 was allocated for administrative purposes. In 1929 the proportion of administrative costs to relief payments issued were proportionately higher than the previous year. This trend was finally reversed in 1930, and in the first five months of 1931, total expenses rose to $15,020.89. However, $12,819.39 was distributed as relief and only $2,201.50 for administration.[11]

On a later visit to Winnebago County in August 1931, Peterson found the situation equally bad in Menasha where the outlays for poor relief were rapidly rising. In 1930, the city had spent $5,036.91 and also had set aside a similar amount for the next year. In the first seven months of 1931, however, the sum spent had already risen to $7,249.35. The new poor commissioner, John Sensenbrenner, had taken office in May 1930. At that time the number of families being cared for was twenty-one but by February 1931 that number had risen to sixty-five. Transients continued to remain a problem. In 1930 there were 986 but by 1931 the number had escalated to 2,291. It cost the city very little to maintain them because they were normally sent to the police station to be "fed, slept and told to move on." The quarters were warm and clean but the lodgers had to provide their own "sleeping accommodations." Heavy paper was spread over the concrete floor and with that for a foundation the men spread their overcoats for a bed using their bundles of extra clothing for pillows. But the numbers of transients kept growing. According to the *The Menasha Record*, "hobo jungles" had sprung up on the west side of town. One of the jungles near the Soo Line yards "had been for many years a gathering place for transients...where they prepare meals, spin yarns and also stay for the night if weather conditions are agreeable."[12]

Peterson soon discovered that outside of a limited amount of miscellaneous charity, the poor commissioner handled all the work himself, although the Red Cross took care of ex-servicemen and the "customary cases." Various church societies collected and distributed clothing. These societies usually telephoned Sensenbrenner so that there was a "semblance" of clearance through his office. There was, nevertheless, considerable duplication of effort on the part of all these societies.[13]

Sensenbrenner made his own investigations which, Peterson thought, "were quite thoro [sic]." He tried to determine how much a family should have to live on then paid just a little bit less so the family would have to "scramble" for the balance. If they complained "too loudly" he often gave them a dollar or two more for the next week. Sensenbrenner issued "money orders" and allowed clients to make their own selections, but cautioned them if they bought what he deemed "luxuries." For a family of two, he allowed $3 per week for groceries and meat. A family of five got $4 to $5 and a family of more than five received $6 to $7 a week. In the matter of rent, the poor commissioner waited until a notice of eviction was served, except in cases of sickness or unusual circumstances. The maximum rent he paid was $25 but the usual was between $18 and $20 a month.[14]

In Neenah, too, the sums for poor relief were rising and proving to be insufficient to cover the increased case load; the figure for 1930 ($5,047.86) had already been eclipsed in the first seven months of 1931 ($5,147.33). The decline in the requests for aid which had been expected in the summer months had not occurred, instead, it doubled from that in the middle of the winter. Many people had not been able to survive through the winter on their own resources by using their savings, mortgaging everything they had and through credit given to them by local businesses; but these were now exhausted and they were forced to seek aid from the poor commissioner. It was estimated that by the end of the year relief costs would soar to over $11,000.[15] These developments occurred, to Peterson's astonishment, despite the fact that she had been convinced Neenah was a wealthy city where industries had been operating "either continuously or on part time" and the city had performed "a great deal of make-work." The amount expended for make-work in 1931 alone came to $40,000, a sum obtained, the mayor, George E. Sande, explained had been raised "by curtailing of expenses and by the use of moneys raised for other purposes for work relief on jobs that were practically all labor..."[16]

Various churches, organization, individuals and clubs did a considerable amount of charity work but they usually consulted with Effie R. Bishop, the Neenah Poor Commissioner, "to get the lay of the land" and there was little duplication of effort. Bishop was unusually conscientious in her work and made very careful inspection of cases, all of which she discussed with her board of supervisors. She spent mornings in her office and afternoons, evenings and Sundays in the field. She also had a secretary who remained in the office at all times. Itemized grocery orders were given so as to secure balanced diets. The basis of determining rent was a "matter of judgment." Usually the rent was paid when the landlord threatened to evict. The maximum came to $25 and the average $20.[17] As in Oshkosh transients were sent to the police station for a night's lodging. Although it was relatively easy to get rid of transients, they or other "kings of the road," kept returning. On the other hand, it was much harder to transfer paupers who had lived in the jurisdiction for a few months into another locality. The usual procedure was to return them to the place of origin. However, local authorities had to exercise restraint as it was illegal to transport paupers out of their areas. In autumn 1932, the police chief of Clintonville arrested C.H. Watts, Neenah's chief, for dumping on Clintonville a pauper family that had resided in Neenah for months. Watts claimed the family was originally from Clintonville and had not been in Neenah the required year to establish residence before becoming a city charge.[18]

Bishop was also head of the local Red Cross. She combined case work with relief and, Peterson thought, was exceptionally capable. The Red Cross served an important function in Neenah, the people having been educated to use it as a clearing house for everything. The government also used the Red Cross for its own charitable purposes.[19] In spring 1932, for instance, the Midwest branch of the Red Cross allocated to the Menasha chapter 150 barrels of flour for distribution as the Menasha Poor Department saw fit. 150 families made use of this flour for a ninety-day period.[20] Later that year 500,000 bales of cotton cloth, made from government cotton, were also turned over to the Menasha chapter.[21]

A report by a probation officer, Margaret A. Thorn, directed to the Winnebago County Board of Supervisors in November 1931 revealed still more personal distress. "Our aid work," Thorn disclosed, "has been greatly increased for there have been constant changes in the family incomes, due to members...being thrown out of work. When we ask the employer what a mother's weekly earnings will be so we will know what to give, he does not know. It may be nothing tomorrow or next week." Consequently, Thorn was at wit's end "to regulate the aid given to meet the needs of the family which may vary greatly from week to week." To Thorn, society seemed to be breaking down. "The number of divorced and deserted mothers and the number of fathers serving prison terms," she pointed out, were increasing with each passing year. Thorn personalized the impact of the Great Depression which had now settled upon the country. "It is indeed heartbreaking," she revealed, "to see the mental anguish and often the physical suffering in these broken homes."[22]

Perhaps the most poignant indication of the wholesale destitution some were driven to during the early years of the Depression centered on Lake Winnebago itself. Ice-fishing had always been a popular sport on the lake and many Oshkosh residents had undoubtedly augmented their diets with fish pulled from its waters. But by 1931, many were using the lake as their personal grocery store. Ignoring any limits imposed by conservation officials, some anglers were willing to extract a month's supply of walleye, northern pike and sturgeon through the ice on a single night and hustle them home to their smokers before wardens could intervene. These environmental abuses became known to state conservation authorities who suggested in 1932 that overnight fishing be banned on the lake. Mayor Taylor Brown of Oshkosh protested by indicating the dire straits in which some citizens found themselves and leveled the mordant verdict that if people could not fish they might starve. The ban was never enacted. Brown and city commissioner, James Skole, secured some twenty nets from the state conservation department so that rough fish could be scooped up. Twice a week city workers raised the nets, brought them to distribution centers and the fish were given out to the needy.[23]

As a recovery year 1931 was a decided failure. Even the *Oshkosh Northwestern*, with a hint of desperation, admitted as much in its final editorial for the year. Nevertheless, the newspaper's exuberance was not completely dulled:

> Times will be better in 1932...We've got to make them better, that's all. They were bad in the year now closing, that's sure, but from any angle it is reasonable to expect that improvement is coming, is here now to some extent, so let's take courage and welcome the first of January with a robust joy.[24]

But it was hard to be joyful when 49 banks had been suspended and 640 companies had failed in the state during 1931 and there were now 7.7% fewer workers in Wisconsin's factories than in December 1930 and 28.6% fewer than in December 1929.[25] Equally telling of a collapsed economy was the cresting rise of delinquent taxes in Winnebago County from $94,248.93 in 1929 to $127,361.72 in 1931. Winnebago County did not enjoy its recovery in 1931; the depression only deepened.[26] What many in the county did not realize was the crisis had not completely bottomed out as yet.

Notes

1. *Oshkosh Northwestern*, January 14, 1931.
2. *MR*, February 11, 1931.
3. *MR*, February 13, 1931. This item carried the bannered legend: "*The Menasha Record* in Cooperation with President Hoover's Emergency Committee for Employment. Washington, D.C., Arthur Woods Chairman."
4. *MR*, April 22, 1931.
5. *Oshkosh Northwestern*, April 2, 1931.

6. *WLMR*, Vol. 11, February 1931, No. 2, p. 1.
7. *Oshkosh Northwestern*, January 14, 1931.
8. Unemployment Relief Administration Records, 1931-1935, Series 1410, Box. No. 4, Folder: Relief Oshkosh, "Distribution of Funds 1928, Overseer of Poor," and see Memorandum of May 20-21-22, 1931, Oshkosh, p. 7. Refer to *Oshkosh: One Hundred Years a City, 1853-1953*, p. 111.
9. SHSW-ARC. Department of Public Welfare. Division of Public Assistance. Unemployment Relief Administration Records, 1931-1933, Series 1410, Box No. 4, Folder: Relief Oshkosh, Memorandum of May 20-21-22, Oshkosh, p. 7.
10. SHSW-ARC. Department of Public Welfare. Division of Public Assistance. Unemployment Relief Administration Records, 1931-1933, Series 1410, Box No. 4, Folder: Relief Oshkosh, Memorandum of May 20-21-22, 1931, Oshkosh, p. 7.
11. SHSW-ARC. Department of Public Welfare, Division of Public Assistance. Unemployment Relief Administration Records, 1931-1933, Series No. 1410, Box No. 4, Folder: Relief Oshkosh, Statistical Report of the Bureau of Family Service, May 28, 1931; see also Folder: Relief Oshkosh, "Distribution of Funds 1931, Overseer of the Poor." Peterson reported that Miss Edna Jean Raddis, "an experienced case worker," was head of the Bureau. Her salary was $2,500 per annum. She had two assistants, one receiving $100 per month and the other, "a stenographer," $75 per month. See earlier Memorandum of May 20-21-22, 1931, Oshkosh, p. 7.
12. Unemployment Relief Administration Records, Series No. 1410, Box No. 3, Folder: Relief Menasha (Winnebago 6), Memorandum of August 21, 1931, Poor Relief, Menasha, Wis. See *MR*, November 5, 1931 for hobo problem.
13. *MR*, January 8, 1932.
14. *MR*, January 7, 1932.
15. Unemployment Relief Administration Records, Series 1410, Box No. 1, Folder: Federal Letters from Cities and Counties, City of Neenah. Copy of letter sent in answer to claim for Federal Aid, July 23, 1932. See also *MR*, July 9, 1931.
16. *MR*, July 9, 1931.
17. Unemployment Relief Administration Records, Series No. 1410, Box No. 3, Folder: Relief Neenah (Winnebago 6), Memorandum of August 20, 1931, Poor Relief, Neenah, Wis.
18. *MR*, September 12, 1932.
19. American Red Cross/Neenah-Menasha Chapters, *Minute Book, 1917-1931, Minute for November 27, 1931*.
20. *MR*, May 18, 1932.
21. *MR*, October 22, 1932.
22. Winnebago County Clerk, *Printed Proceedings of the County Board of Supervisors*, Winnebago Series, Box 1, No.1, Annual November Session, 1931,Rep. No.37, pp. 86-87.
23. Michael Goc, *Oshkosh: 150 Years*, pp. 83-84.
24. *Oshkosh Northwestern*, December 31, 1931.
25. *WLMR*, Vol. 12, January 1932, No. 1, p. 1; Vol. 13, January 1933, no. 1, p. 28.
26. *MR*, March 25, 1931.

Chapter 4

1932: The Depths of Depression

On Monday, January 18, 1932, arguably the most famous horror film ever made, *Frankenstein*, began playing in Oshkosh. Loosely based on Mary Shelley's novel, it told the story of Baron Frankenstein's use of science to create a living creature out of body parts of the dead. The experiment, at first successful, went awry and mayhem and murder followed. The film had a connection with Oshkosh. Its producer, Carl Laemmele, had once been a manager of a men's clothing store on Main Street before going into the entertainment business and eventually ending up in Hollywood as a founder of Universal Studios which made *Frankenstein*. A number of people pointed out the extraordinary links between the film and the Great Depression. Like Frankenstein's creature which brought only disappointment, the technology that had grown out of science was doing the same. Machines could produce almost all of the material goods needed but few could afford them. Advances in agriculture led to bountiful harvests and yet people were starving. Men were willing to work for pennies an hour but no business could afford to hire them. The world seemed to have turned upside down and the hopeful notion that science would in time solve everything had been shattered, even in Winnebago County.[1]

The tragic economic decline forced the state legislatures, over the objections of many important businessmen, to enact, early in 1932 the first unemployment compensation act in American history. The law was signed into effect by Governor La Follette on January 28. It was but a modest gesture. The terms required any employer of ten or more persons to deposit 2% of the company's payroll in the employer's state-controlled account. Once total deposits reached $55 for each employee, the company's contribution was reduced to one percent. Contributions remained at that level until individual accounts reach $75 per employee at which time the company's contribution ceased. Workers could obtain benefits for a maximum of ten weeks at the rate of 50% of their average weekly wage. However, compensation could not exceed $10 a week.

The plan took four years to ease into operation. In order to overcome opposition La Follette had to agree that it should at first be voluntary and would become compulsory only if an insufficient number of employers adopted it. Inasmuch as this was the case, the act became compulsory in 1933. Payments into the fund began to be made in 1934 and the first compensation check was not paid until August 1936.[2]

At the same time La Follette managed to get the legislature to pass an emergency relief act appropriating $8 million (he had requested $17 million) to be used for direct relief and public works projects, as well as for a reduction in property taxes. The act also established a forestry program in northern Wisconsin. But, unfortunately, these measures had little impact upon rapidly rising unemployment.[3]

The Emergency Relief Act prompted La Follette to send a memorandum to county, city, town and village clerks to make certain in the matter of local relief, which amounted to over $5 million, that "competent persons be placed in charge of such relief work, that careful investigation of applicants be made, that proper case records be kept, and that a family budget sufficient for health and decency be provided.[4] A handbook dealing with the administration of relief was to be sent immediately from the Industrial Commission which was charged with the distribution of funds. La Follette's letter forced local governments to set aside the casual procedures they had followed in the past.

As 1932 advanced, matters grew worse. Farm income fell below that of 1910 in spite of an increase in production of about 28% since pre-war days.[5] Industrial figures were equally bad. By May, factory employment was 36% lower than in May 1930; corresponding factory employee payrolls aggregated 59.1% less than for May 1930; average per capita weekly earnings of factory workers amounted to $15.61 in contrast with $24.79 two years earlier.[6] By summer of 1932 stock prices were 72% below the lowest levels of 1929.[7]

The consequences were quickly discernible in Winnebago County. In Menasha the figures for poor relief were alarming. The budget appropriation for the year was $15,000, but by the end of June $11,600.90 had already been expended; of this sum, $5,000 alone had been spent in June. Moreover, the amount paid by the city for direct labor in lieu of direct poor relief was $5,436.05. Private funds for poor relief were by now exhausted. John Jedwabny, the city clerk, declared, "if our expenditures for poor relief from now [June 30, 1932] until the end of the year continue to increase at the present rate, our budget appropriation together with other sources of revenue for that purpose, will be about $20,000 short. Our condition is becoming acute, with the expenditures for rent increasing daily and the coming winter months near at hand."[8]

In Neenah, too, the figures were disturbing. From January to July 1, 1932, $15,405 had been disbursed on poor relief and $21,300 on work relief. It was estimated that $13,000 more (direct poor relief) and $20,000 more (work relief) would have to be spent during the remainder of the year. Mayor George Sande explained that Neenah had begun in 1932 "with a surplus from the previous years of $63,520.75, all of which moneys have been expended on work relief projects to date...". He then went on to say that "the revenues from Income Taxes for the years 1929-1930 and 1931 averaged $104,093.41 and that the amount to be received this year is less than $55,000 and the estimate for 1933 is only $20,000." [9] In an attempt to save some money, the mayor, aldermen, city clerk, treasurer and department heads as well as members of the police and fire departments all volunteered to take a 10% pay cut beginning on August 1, 1932. All employees paid on an hourly basis had their workdays reduced from nine to eight hours but the rate of pay per hour was not cut.[10]

It was in Oshkosh, however, that the situation was truly frightening. On July 23, 1932 the mayor and the city clerk declared:

> Our relief expenditures during a normal year have averaged around $14,000 per year. We are at the present time expending considerably over $20,000 per month for relief. Our poor budget this year was $45,000, which was an increase of $25,000 over last year. However, this year's budget of $45,000 was used up for poor relief before the end of the first three months. We received $40,108 from the State of Wisconsin which was our relief allotment according to population, and this amount was used up in less than two months. We have expended up to July 1st, $86,699.41. During the month of July we spent $19,525.47 up to July 19th. It looks quite probably that we will have to expend considerably over $100,000 during the balance of the year. Our poor department expenses would have been still greater this year, had we not expended $50,000 in storm sewer work, doing practically all of the work by hand.

Moreover, they went on, "The $60,000 which was raised for private relief funds in our city is exhausted and the families which were formerly taken care of by the Bureau of Family Service and the Catholic Apostolate are now being carried mostly by the city poor department." They concluded by stating: "We are taking care of 973 families or 4,865 persons, and in case our municipality would have to curtail relief, there would be much distress and suffering."[11]

The impact of these figures meant that feeding the unemployed was taking precedence over all other kinds of charity. When, for example, Mowry Smith, president of the Menasha Woodenware Corporation, wrote to George Gaylord, president of the Menasha Products Company, requesting his usual subvention for the Boy Scouts, Gaylord replied that he could not contribute. "I am already," he responded, "giving more than I really can afford to do to help people, in terms of the primary necessities, and regardless of the merits of the Boy Scouts, after all, it is not a question here whether the boys get three meals a day or not."[12]

By late May, the Great Depression was affecting almost everybody in Winnebago County. At First Lutheran Church in Oshkosh parishioners could no longer afford to make even modest offerings at weekly Sunday services. Some were so embarrassed by their failure to contribute that they wanted to leave the church entirely. The Reverend E.A. Koch would not hear of it. "What kind of church would abandon someone when times became difficult," he countered. Indeed, the pastor and his family were without funds as the church had no money to pay his salary for months at a time, but as he explained later on, "the grocer just continued to carry us."[13]

Retail establishments were also much affected in mid-summer 1932 by the Depression. In Neenah, the Krueger Hardware and Furniture Company was obliged to cut costs because of a decline in sales volume and it did so by cutting wages by reducing the scheduled hours of its employees and trimming the monthly salaries of its owners from $200 to $150.[14] Howard Angermeyer, whose family ran a plumbing outfit in Neenah, recalled that there was real poverty evident at his school, for many of the students brought school lunches composed entirely of potato peels. "Potato-peel eaters were from the poorest families," he explained.[15]

Tom Marcourt remembered well the dismal financial prospects for workers in Oshkosh in autumn 1932. His father managed the Oshkosh Millwork Company and was deeply concerned about laying off his workers. In an attempt to preserve jobs, he cut back hours so that workers would all remain on the payroll, even if the weekly check was meager. It certainly was low; the workers made only twenty cents per hour. But it was better than nothing at all.[16]

Helen Burr, whose father was a truck driver for Winnebago County, recalled that in late 1932 the south side of Oshkosh was feeling the pangs of suffering. At South Park Elementary School, many children were shabbily dressed and packed small school lunches composed of bread coated with lard and sprinkled with salt. She was lucky, however, as the family worked ten acres of land on the south end of the city and grew much of their own food.[17] Betty Patterson of Oshkosh remembered with pain a day in October 1932 when her father, a sales representative for Bethlehem Steel Company, lost his job, lost whatever money he had saved, and was forced to sell his automobile to a local grocery store owner in return for food.[18]

These stories of quiet desperation were being duplicated all over the county. Everywhere local governments were being overwhelmed by demands for relief. Under tremendous pressure, therefore, President Hoover, on July 21, 1932, signed an Emergency Relief and Construction Act which furnished $2 billion in loans to the states for public works and $300 million for relief. Twelve million dollars for relief was given to Wisconsin to be distributed by the Industrial Commission to counties and cities in accordance with their needs and actual expenditures; but with so many unemployed by this time it was far from adequate.[19]

As summer faded into autumn, politics again began to assume the foreground of attention. Popular annoyance with the Republicans about the Depression was giving the party difficulties. Moreover, the split between Progressives and Stalwarts within the party was widening. With the coming primary, the division became wider: the Progressives attempted to ruin the Stalwarts by tarring them with Hoover's unpopularity and asserting that they were representatives of the rich. But the Progressives themselves were in difficulty. They had always depended upon liberal Democrats (who often abandoned the conservative stance of their party) to help defeat the Stalwarts in the primary elections by voting

Progressive. But the growing popularity of Franklin D. Roosevelt was attracting these Democrats back into their own party. La Follette's opponent, former Governor Walter Kohler, ran a vigorous campaign. "No one will go hungry in this state if I am elected," he told supporters at a rally in Neenah. The biggest problem he insisted was unemployment. About 200,000 people were out of work and an equal number were working only part-time. If elected his first responsibility, therefore, would be to save people from starving and then aid them to save their homes and farms. Twenty-five percent of real property in Wisconsin was now tax delinquent, he noted. What was to be done? Here Kohler abandoned his former *laissez-faire* attitude in order to espouse government involvement by favoring the levying of additional income taxes if necessary and establishing municipal projects to provide work. Industry too should help by trying to provide one more day of work each week. The Depression had reached its lowest point, he asserted. The trend would now be upward.[20]

The primary held on September 20 was a disaster for the Progressives. Kohler received 414,575 votes to La Follette's 319,884, thus seeming to ensure his election in November. In Winnebago County, La Follette did very poorly, obtaining only 6,629 votes to Kohler's 12,971.[21]

The number of people applying for aid put a severe strain on the Oshkosh poor department and it was necessary to hire investigators to deal with the increased load. Examinations were held in early November and the fifteen persons receiving the highest grades were interviewed by Edith Foster of the Wisconsin Industrial Commission who chose seven, all of whom were women. They were to receive $90 a month and pay all their own expenses such as transportation. Each investigator was to handle a district comprising 150 families and personal calls were to be made on the families at least once every two weeks. The investigators were to give out poor department vouchers for food and rent at the time of their visits and it was hoped that this would take the crowd away from the poor commissioner's office at the city hall. Mrs. Eugene G. Williams, who was to be the chief of the investigators, was given a salary of $130 a month and Ernest P. Schlerf, hired as a "special" agent, was to take charge of transient shelters at a salary of $100 per month. The old post office building was renovated somewhat as a transient shelter and the Oshkosh city government obtained cots and blankets from the state militia.[22]

Unavoidably dubbed, "Hotel Depression," the transient shelter's formal name was the Good Will Home, and it served food and housed an average of twenty transients a day, and on one "peak day," according to assistant supervisor Theodore Engelke, "sixty-three men were given care." According to one of the directors, the Reverend Henry F. Polley, the house was intended primarily for Oshkosh's unemployed single men. The principal purpose behind the home was to insure that "young Oshkosh men who find themselves 'up against it' from turning into bums," with the ideal being to establish a reputation for Oshkosh as a place "with no local bums." The "guests" performed a variety of menial chores to maintain the center and most stayed but a handful of days. Anyone who had "destinations in view" were urged to hurry along, "but those who [had] no homes nor any place to go [were] given their leisure in making a departure."[23]

Up the road in Menasha there were indications that respectable citizens were tiring of efforts to provide relief, particularly if it conflicted with their own interests. Residents in the vicinity of the Jefferson School petitioned the mayor and common council to scrap the idea of turning it into a poor house because it would decrease the value of surrounding properties and would "bring undesirable people into the neighborhood.[24]

At the same time the finance committee of the Oshkosh School Board reduced the budget from the 1932 figure of $547,733 to $453,000 for 1933. It also ordered yet another 10% reduction for teachers in their 1933-1934 contract. By way of further explanation, however, the chair of the finance committee asserted that the increased purchasing power of the dollar at this time still left the teachers with higher actual salaries. McGowan's Coffee Shop in Oshkosh, for example, advertised a Sunday dinner for 75 cents which offered soup, roast turkey or duck, fricassee of chicken with dumplings, T-bone steak, french-fried potatoes, kumquat salad, buttered squash, French rolls, lemon sherbet, coffee, tea, milk, apple, mince, pumpkin pie or ice-cream.[25]

Reductions in salaries were practically the order of the day. The Winnebago County Board of Supervisors voted a 10% cut in salaries for all county officials and employees to take place after January 1, 1933. The saving amounted to $6,872.94 a year. Although the Oshkosh School Board was the most draconian in its budgetary cutbacks, Neenah and Menasha could not avoid the inevitable scourge. In Neenah the school board cut salaries by 7.5% across the board and some teacher contracts were not renewed. In Menasha, former high school band leader, Lawrence Kraft, remembered the hard times as well. There the vocal department and orchestra were discontinued, eliminating the two positions in the music department. Others, Kraft surmised, must have been let go as well. However, the band "was quite popular" at Menasha High School, so Kraft was able to keep his job.[26]

In the Oshkosh municipal government quite a flap was caused by the pressure to reduce city employee salaries. Earlier, most workers saw their annual salaries scaled by 10%, and as the year was coming to a close, it was being suggested that another similar reduction was required. Apparently, Mayor Brown and several of the councilmen, most conspicuously, Henry Hagene, had spared themselves the first cut and were waxing belligerently about resisting the next installment. According to one report, Mayor Brown grudgingly yielded to the insistent demand for a 10% reduction of his $5000 a year salary but announced he would cease making any further donations to charity. Hagene went on record for flatly refusing to accept a cut in his $4500 annual salary. In rather florid imagery, *The Fox Valley Free Press* headlined an editorial with an invidious comparison to Marie-Antoinette, trumpeting, "'Let Them Eat Cake Then' Is Bourbon Philosophy of Lord Brown and Duke Hagene."[27]

By late fall elections were approaching and Hoover, despite all of his best efforts, was facing a potential political disaster which turned into a real one on November 8 when national and local elections swept Roosevelt to the presidency and destroyed Republican influence in Congress and the Wisconsin Legislature.[28] In Wisconsin the Democratic mayor of Madison, Albert J. Schmedemann, defeated Walter Kohler by 590,114 votes to 470,805 to become the new governor. In Winnebago County, however, the figures were far from clear cut. The county chose Roosevelt for president but Kohler for governor. The Democrat, Michael K. Reilly, a veteran politician from Fond du Lac who had also served in the 63rd and 64th Congresses, won the Sixth Congressional district in a close contest over his Republican rival Louis J. Fellenz. Winnebago County also threw out its Republican representatives in the State Assembly and chose instead two Democrats, William Grimes and Ray Novotny. It was not, however, a complete rout: 69 year-old Merritt F. White, a Republican, maintained his seat (held since 1923) in the Wisconsin Senate for Calumet and Winnebago counties.[29]

Once the excitement generated by the election had subsided, the public interest turned to mundane matters, such as publicly posting the names of people who received relief. Complaints about this practice had been sent to Madison and evoked a strong rebuke from Florence Peterson of the Industrial Commission, warning that Oshkosh would not get any federal relief money if it continued to do so. Some councilmen wanted to persist in posting names, but Mayor Brown suggested a compromise. Such lists, he maintained, ought to be accessible to anyone who might want to examine them but should not be posted publicly "where they might be perused by the morbidly curious in search of material for gossip." The practice was thereupon abandoned.[30]

As the year ended, the *Oshkosh Northwestern* came out with an editorial that was almost equally sanguine as those of the previous two Decembers:

> The old year, 1932, failed to bring back the prosperity that was expected, and there are tragic memories of disappointment and distress that will never be fully erased. But foundations were laid for a return to normal conditions, and 1933, unless all signs fail, will come upon the scene with new hopes, aspirations and promises.[31]

What foundations were laid, were not specified and certainly there were no indications of such from local businessmen who at best had a "hunch" that 1933 might show improvement. After all, how could it get any worse? By now they had become cautious in making any definitive predictions as they remembered that "favorable signs" they have talked about in 1930, 1931, and 1932 had not come to fruition. They concluded that nothing was to be gained by creating false hopes.[32] As there had been another 67 bank suspensions and 788 commercial failures in Wisconsin during the year hopes were tenebrous.[33] Added to the gloomy prospects was the news that the Oshkosh Community Welfare Fund collected only $15,680 of the $24,000 goal it had set for itself.[34]

Notes

1. *Oshkosh Northwestern*, January 18, 1932.
2. James I. Clark, *Wisconsin Meets the Great Depression*. (Madison: State Historical Society of Wisconsin, 1956), pp. 10-11; Glad, *War, a New Era, and Depression*, pp. 395; Robert W. Ozanne, *The Labor Movement in Wisconsin*. (Madison: State Historical Society of Wisconsin, 1984), p. 131.
3. Glad, *War, a New Era and Depression*, pp. 395-96.
4. Unemployment Relief Administration Records, 1931-1933, Series No. 1410, Box No. 1, Folder: Relief Gov. La Follette, memorandum of February 15, 1932 by Governor La Follette to County, Town, Village and City Clerks.
5. "Farm Prices and Income since 1929," *WBB*, 1933, p. 139.
6. *WLMR*, Vol. 12, June 1932, No. 6, p. 1.
7. Glad, *War, a New Era, and Depression*, p. 350.
8. Unemployment Relief Administration Records, Series No. 1410, Box No. 1, Folder: Federal--Letters from Cities & Counties, Memorandum of expenditures for direct poor relief and poor labor in the city of Menasha as of June 30, 1932. See also, *MR*, July 6, 1932.
9. Letter of July 23, 1932 by Sande in answer to claim for federal aid.
10. *MR*, August 19, 1932.
11. *MR*, August 19, 1932, Memorandum of July 23, 1932 by the Mayor and City Clerk of Oshkosh.
12. UWO-ARC. M. Smith, Personal Correspondence, November 1919 to May 1932, Box No. 1, Letter of May 24, 1932 by George Gaylord to Mowry Smith.
13. *Oshkosh Northwestern*, July 23-24, 1978, weekend edition.
14. Tru-Value Hardware Archives/Neenah. H.F. Krueger Hardware & Furniture Company. Record Book, regular meeting of July 23, 1932, pp. 50-51.
15. UWO/Archives. Collection of Interviews dealing with the Great Depression and Prohibition conducted by Paul Stellpflug. Oral Interview with Howard Angermeyer, February 21, 1995.
16. UWO/Archives. Collection of Interviews dealing with the Great Depression and Prohibition, Oral Interview with Tom Marcourt, February 20, 1995.
17. UWO/Archives. Collection of Interviews dealing with the Great Depression and Prohibition, Oral Interview with Helen Lord Burr, February 22, 1995.
18. UWO/Archives. Collection of Interviews dealing with the Great Depression and Prohibition, Oral Interview with Betty Patterson, March 24, 1995.
19. *WBB*, 1933, p. 336.
20. *MR*, October 26, 1932.
21. *WBB* 1933, p. 515. Also note that Albert B. Steadman (Dem.) received 1,858 votes.
22. *Oshkosh Northwestern*, November 2, 1932 and November 4, 1932.
23. Although the need for a shelter did not disappear the poor center, totally reliant upon private donations, was unable to sustain itself into the following year. See *Oshkosh Northwestern*, February 13, 1932; *Fox Valley Free Press*, December 19, 1932. The *Fox Valley Free Press* was the successor of the *Fox Valley Square Dealer*, a weekly launched on December 9, 1931 and ending on May 21, 1932. The new paper's volatile editor, Roland Senn, wielded a vitriolic pen and the paper became a casualty of a libel suit issued against Senn. The *Free Press*, under the equally acerbic but infinitely more restrained editor, Lynn Peavy, was another weekly with hopes of becoming a bi-weekly, and it

printed its inaugural edition on August 5, 1932 and closed shop on November, 1939. Unfortunately, many editions spanning this seven-year period are no longer available for review. Both papers were predicated upon a conviction that an alternative view of matters was needed as the dominant news organ, the *Oshkosh Northwestern*, was too cozy with the mayoral administration of Taylor Brown.

24. UWO-ARC. City of Menasha, Office of the City Clerk, Petitions to the Common Council, 1860-1936. Box 3, Folder 4: Petitions 1929-1936.
25. *Oshkosh Northwestern*, November 26, 1932. The School Board had some other surprises in store for 1933 in order to slash its budget. Beginning in 1933 the system would dispense with the practice of permitting 4 year-olds to attend school. Pushing the entrance age up a year translated into the dismissal of eight teachers, all of whom were women. Classes were combined and supervisors and principals descended into the instructional ranks. Moreover, teachers were moved from annual to monthly contracts for fear that the system might come up short in payments. Also, married women teachers were not slated for rehire in 1933, the assumption being that their husbands could support them. In 1931 the average annual teacher salary had been $1,690. In 1933 that figure squared at $1,362. See Michael Goc, *Oshkosh: 150 Years*, p. 83.
26. *MR*, May 5, 1932 and July 28, 1932.
27. *Fox Valley Free Press*, December 9, 1932.
28. James R. Chiles, "Bang! Went the Doors on Every Bank in America," *Smithsonian* (April 1997), Vol.28, No. 1, p. 124.
29. *Oshkosh Northwestern*, November 19, 1932.
30. *Oshkosh Northwestern*, November 19, 1932. In Menasha the practice had been discouraged by the mayor. See *MR*, July 6, 1932.
31. *Oshkosh Northwestern*, December 31, 1932.
32. *Oshkosh Northwestern*, December 31, 1932.
33. *WLMR*, Vol. 13, January 1933, No.1, pp. 12-14.
34. *Oshkosh Northwestern*, December 31, 1932.

Chapter 5

1933: The Federal Government Weighs In

On January 2, 1933, Albert J. Schmedemann was inaugurated as governor of Wisconsin. Schmedemann, 68, was the first Democrat to hold the office in thirty-eight years. By now the Depression had reached what seemed to be its nadir. The average weekly wage in Oshkosh was $8.72 and $16.12 in Neenah and Menasha.[1] This decline in wages was also underscored in Oshkosh by the experience of the Leach Company, a manufacturer of garbage trucks. In 1930 the company payroll stood at $64,868; by 1933 it had plunged to $7,873.[2]

The rise in hardship accompanying these figures meant increasing numbers of people were looking for help. The County Board was now forced to act on a resolution made the previous November to choose a county supervisor of outdoor public relief.[3] Eighty-eight people applied for the appointment. The candidates were required to have several qualifications, such as the ability to keep accurate records, to delve "behind the surface" of the applicant for aid as well as a sense of empathy, tempered by an attitude of being "hard-boiled" in order to deal with "professional paupers."[4] Early in January, Louis J. Howman of Neenah was selected with a salary of $1,500 per year. Howman, 42, was a graduate of Neenah High School and had attended Valparaiso University for one term. Married and the father of three sons, he knew well the problem of being out of work, having been employed "at intervals, a day or two at a time." Howman had no training in poor relief matters but the committee that chose him favored an unemployed person rather than one with experience. A member of the Board objected saying that the appointment should have gone to a qualified man. It appeared to him that "extraordinary talent" could be secured "in these times at $100 a month, as shown by the caliber of the majority of the applicants."[5]

The question of work was of uppermost importance in the minds of every citizen and politician, some of whom advocated schemes to increase employment that were quite fanciful. William Grimes, state assemblyman recently elected to the Second District, proposed to the Neenah Club a plan to lend $500 to every individual farmer and homeowner in the state with the provision that the money be spent for property improvements. This scheme, he said, would provide work for everybody and end the Depression almost overnight. Federal and state governments and community banks would participate jointly in the loans. Borrowers would be charged at the rate of one-percent, the state would pay one-percent, the federal government one percent for the three-percent interest-bearing bonds which would be issued to finance the loans. Borrowers who failed to spend the money on improvement would be given jail sentences. The silliness of the scheme was readily apparent to everyone except its author. No money would be given to millions of ordinary workers who did not own property, thus making them second-class citizens. Moreover, it would require a legion of bureaucrats to administer. Nevertheless, despite its apparent faults, Grimes intended to put it before Schmedemann.[6]

Those who hoped the new administration would bring better times were destined to be disappointed. Schmedemann turned out to be a timid incompetent who was reluctant to initiate economic reforms. Moreover, a new problem in the form of labor strikes began to add to the government's difficulties. The first big one was the milk strike, chiefly centered in the Fox River Valley.

Agriculture remained an integral part of the Wisconsin's economy and an important part of agriculture was the dairy industry. In 1930 Wisconsin ranked as the sixteenth state in farm population and farm acreage, but eighth in value of farm property, thirteenth in the value of farm crops, and first in dairy and related livestock products. Of Wisconsin's 181,767 farms above 125,000 were classified as dairy farms.[7] During the 1920s, the milk price index declined from nearly $3.00 per hundredweight (1919) to about $2.00 in 1929. As consumers cut down on milk purchases in consequence of the Depression further decline set in so that the price per hundredweight was less than $1.00 in 1932.[8] In 1929 Wisconsin farm prices averaged 55% above the 1914 level. In 1931 they averaged 10% below the 1914 level, a net decline of 42%. By June 1932, the Wisconsin index of farm prices had declined to a level of 60% of 1914, a drop of over 61% from the average of 1929. This was the most drastic decline in agricultural prices of which there was any record. Unusually severe and prolonged drought prevailed in many parts of Wisconsin during 1930, 1931, and 1932. Farm income closely followed the trend of farm prices; in 1929 it was $438 million. It dipped to $190 million in 1932.[9]

Other sectors of agriculture were also severely shaken by the Depression. The result was the establishment of a number of groups whose aim was to help farmers. Beginning in Iowa farmers organized the National Farm Holiday Association which withheld farm products from markets in hope of securing higher prices. The idea quickly spread to Wisconsin where in September 1932 a branch of the Holiday Association was formed in Marshfield which endorsed the use of strikes to obtain its goals. Its head was a radical, Arnold Gilbert, a Dunn County farmer, who was supposed to have said, "We'll solve our problems with bayonets, and I don't mean maybe.[10] Within a few months the Wisconsin group claimed 130,000 members.

Among the most aggressive of the farmers were members of the Wisconsin Cooperative Milk Pool. The president of the Pool, Walter M. Singler, grew up near Shiocton in Outagamie County. A tall, powerful man, addicted to flashy clothes, Singler was noted for his persuasive speeches. He and his organization would give Governor Schmedemann his first headache. At a meeting in Appleton Singler got the Pool to call a strike for February 15. The aim was to force the price of milk upwards to at least $1.40 per hundredweight.[11]

As only 4 percent of the population made its living by farming in Winnebago County it appeared that the region would not be very much affected. Thus, Outagamie County became the strike stronghold. Nevertheless, when the strike erupted on the morning of February 15 its vigor in Winnebago County caught many by surprise.[12] And the strike only continued to grow in the passing days. Despite the winter weather farmers stood guard along roads leading to the creameries to prevent deliveries; elsewhere the milk was seized and dumped.[13] In an attempt to keep order and permit deliveries special sheriff's deputies patrolled the highways and in some cases rode along in trucks as drivers carrying consignments to creameries and dairies. Tempers flared when on February 17 it was reported that a random shot was fired at a truck attempting to deliver milk in Neenah.[14] Despite the promising start the strike began to ebb in Winnebago County and within a few days there was little interference with milk deliveries. The strike continued, however, to go on strongly in Outagamie County.[15]

While the strike was in progress some farmers began to hint that it should be called off until the incoming president would have time to deal with the problems afflicting agriculture. This point of view won out and on February 22 the executive committee of the Wisconsin Milk Pool, including Singler, held a meeting in Madison and adopted a resolution recommending to the Pool that it declare a truce to last until May 1. Arbitration ended this milk strike in May but the problem of depressed agricultural prices was by no means at an end.[16]

With the temporary calming of the milk strike, Schmedemann faced a far greater crisis; a potential collapse of banking in Wisconsin. The problem was not peculiar to the state but was nationwide. Banks were failing everywhere and, consequently, people who still had savings withdrew them and kept them at home.[17]

In Oshkosh, for example, the Paine Thrift Bank closed on January 24, 1933. The following day the City National Bank shut down. Crowds gathered in the streets. At noon the next day, Mayor George Oaks issued a proclamation "calling on all banks and business houses not dealing in necessities of life to call a holiday for the remainder of the week." Oaks said that the proclamation was made "as a matter of policy to afford opportunity for the situation to quiet itself so that people will use their better judgment rather than snap judgment."[18]

The situation soon worsened. Depositors everywhere continued to withdraw their money and in an attempt to stave off complete failure state governments contemplated closing banks. It appeared that the only way to avoid a total banking collapse in Wisconsin was for Schmedemann to do something decisive.

After consulting with the state banking review board he decided upon a course of action. On March 3, Thomas J. O'Malley, acting governor (Schmedemann was in Washington D.C. to attend the inauguration of Roosevelt), issued a proclamation closing all banks immediately and lasting until midnight, Thursday, March 16.[19]

The next day Franklin Delano Roosevelt was inaugurated as president. By this time somewhere between 13 and 14 million American were out of work. That translated into something like 40 million people who could not count on a regular source of income. More than a million hoboes rode the rails on freight cars and according to the Children's Bureau a quarter million were boys and girls, and there were many thousands more who hitchhiked about the country, all looking for jobs.[20] Living conditions were at an all time low; poor housing, not enough food, minimal health care, and insufficient clothing. Even for those who were employed, millions were underpaid or worked only part time. In early 1933 families were losing their homes at a rate of more than a thousand a day. Investment in new residential non-farm construction declined from $3.6 billion in 1929 to $0.5 billion in 1933.[21]

Roosevelt knew that the hopes of millions of depositors and the regeneration of the economy depended upon the return of confidence in the banking system. But that could only occur if banks were investigated by government officials and pronounced safe. The president's first act, therefore, was to order a short banking holiday from Monday, March 6 to Thursday, March 9.[22]

More time was needed for the investigation so the opening date was delayed to Monday, March 13. But how was it possible for the government to inspect the books of nearly 18,000 banks throughout the country in a week? The only route for the government was to depend upon the good judgment of local bankers themselves and to interpret the requirement for soundness as liberally as possible. It was a risky thing to do but it worked.[23]

On Wednesday, March 15, at 9:00 a.m., Menasha's two banks (Bank of Menasha and First National Bank of Menasha) were allowed to re-open. There was no evidence of unrest in Menasha during the holiday, although there was noticeable inconvenience. The shut-down had not been absolute. Banks had still been open to exchange large currency into smaller denominations or coins and customers had been allowed to check their safety deposit boxes.[24]

In Neenah the two established banks, the Neenah State Bank and the National Manufacturers Bank resumed operation on March 15. Both managed to pay depositors over time and reimburse investors in full. While the Neenah State Bank was eventually compelled to liquidate, the National Manufacturers Bank plodded onward toward solvency. In rural Winneconne, banks were plagued by a languishing farm economy and the lack of developing businesses in the town. As elsewhere, the assets became so severely strained that the Union Bank in the village was forced to declare a seven-day holiday in late January 1933. When it opened its doors it implemented a "deferred payment plan," meaning that depositors would be permitted to withdraw only 70% of their assets on demand, with the remainder doled out over a five-year period. Even these stringent measures were not enough to keep the bank afloat. It closed for good on July 27, 1933. The following year a branch of the Farmer's Bank of Omro opened a branch in Winneconne, occupying the old offices of the Union Bank. With federal assistance, and administered by the state banking commission, Winneconne villagers could do banking in their own town.[25]

While the bank holiday was in progress, the problem faced by dairy farmers led to calls for a second milk strike. On March 8 a public meeting was held in the S.A. Cook Armory in Menasha. About 2,500 people succeeded in wedging themselves into the building while another 200 to 300 congregated outside to hear a "pro and con milk debate" arranged by a group of Winnebago County farmers who had invited Singler and other leaders to speak. The audience was decidedly radical and there were calls for the confiscation of property and the seizure of the state government. Despite the fiery rhetoric nothing was decided upon.[26] But just as the dairy farmers were planning to revive the milk strike, President Roosevelt was about to establish what many people thought was to be one of the most famous agencies, the Civilian Conservation Corps (CCC), designed to relieve youthful unemployment and provide for a long-range conservation program.

Roosevelt began his political career as a senator in the New York state legislature in 1910. As he liked to list his occupation as a gentleman farmer it was not surprising that his first appointment was a chair of the state's forest, fish and game committee. The passion for the rural environment lasted for the remainder of his life. When he became governor in 1929 and faced soaring unemployment he undertook with the help of the legislature a broad program of reforestation which put thousands of men to work. Even with emergency legislation Roosevelt came to realize that the state could not keep pace with growing unemployment. Furthermore, he had come to believe that local, county and state agencies could not manage the problem alone.

In the early nineteenth century the vast extent of natural resources such as forests and minerals in proportion to the population of the United States meant that the idea of conservation was irrelevant. The emphasis was upon the exploitation of these resources and to make them cheaply and readily available to advance the settlement of the nation. It was not until the close of the century when forests began to disappear that these assumptions came under questioning.

Wisconsin had a special interest in the emerging conservation movement for it was one of the state's most famous citizens, Carl Schurz, who was one of its pioneers. In his first report as Secretary of the Interior, presented in 1877, he urged the appointment of a commission to study the practices adopted in other countries for the preservation of forests. Schurz was immediately attacked in Congress and by many lumbermen. These attacks were so effective that even the pitifully small sums available to the Department of the Interior for policing national forests against timber thieves were actually reduced. Less than one million acres of timber land remained in a state once famous for its forests.

By the first decade of the twentieth-century, however, a conservation agenda was emerging through the interests of consumers aroused by the rising prices of production, a resentment of the waste involved and the recognition of the public's dependence upon its natural resources. Moreover, a new president, Theodore Roosevelt, believed that the husbanding of natural resources was essential to the character-building of American manhood. This led to the formation of societies for the preservation of forests and wildlife.[27]

When he was nominated for President by the Democrats in July 1932, Franklin Roosevelt made an acceptance speech in which he stated in part that public works were a means of alleviating conservation problems by using the unemployed for reforestation and related work. There were examples to be followed, for such programs had been established by 1932 in many European countries. In America, too, a series of forest camps using unemployed men were being developed by the U.S. Forestry Service in California, Oregon and Washington. Thus, Roosevelt's keenness for conservation, his work in New York, the example of several European countries and the U.S. Forestry Service pressed the President toward the idea of a national conservation program that, he believed, would at once save the land and put hundreds of thousands to work.

On March 21, 1933 the President addressed the 73rd Congress, then in emergency session, concerning the topic of unemployment relief. "I propose," he began, "to create a Civilian Conservation Corps to be used in simple work, not interfering with normal employment and confining itself to forestry, the prevention of soil erosion, flood control and similar projects." Then days later the Congress passed the Emergency Conservation Work Act which set up an agency called the Civilian Conservation Corps (CCC).[28]

The Corps, composed of 250,000 men, primarily but not exclusively between the ages of 18 and 25, enlisted for six months (re-enlistments for two more six-month periods were permitted). The recruits were to be unmarried, unemployed and from families on relief.[29] Each man had to be over 60 inches but under 78 inches in height, more than 107 pounds in weight and possessing at least "three serviceable natural masticating teeth both above and below." Any man wishing to enroll could obtain an application form at a local welfare organization. The recruit received $30 a month, of which $23 were to be allotted to their dependents. Each worker also received food, clothing, shelter and medical care.[30]

On April 5, Roosevelt appointed Robert Fechner as director of the agency at an annual salary of $12,000 and expenses. Born in 1876 in Tennessee, he grew up in Georgia. Fechner quit school at sixteen and eventually became a machinist's apprentice and subsequently was involved in union activities. By 1914 he was a vice-president of the American Federation of Labor (AFL). During World War I Fechner went to Washington as a special advisor on labor policy and at this time he met Roosevelt. The two became friends and in the election of 1932 Fechner worked hard to swing the Machinists Union to the Democrats. Thus when the president was considering a labor leader to head the CCC, the affable, hard-working, honest Fechner came readily to mind.

The Federal Government Weighs In

Fechner was assisted by several government departments. The Department of Labor selected the men; the War Department clothed, fed, housed and transported them; the Departments of Agriculture and Interior chose the work projects and supervised the work. It soon became apparent that Agriculture and Interior had neither the staff, equipment nor experience to administer the camps. Realizing that something had to be done and that the War Department, especially its chief branch, the army, alone had the necessary background and resources to do it, Roosevelt enlarged the army's role to assume, under the general supervision of Fechner, complete and permanent control of the CCC project.[31]

Although the act specified that there should be no discrimination on account of race, color or creed, the CCC suffered from the racist and bigoted ideas of many army officers who dominated it. The most blatant example was General George Van Horne Mosley who controlled CCC activities in the south. He believed blacks were inferior both biologically and socially and treated them accordingly. Mosley was also anti-semitic calling for the "sterilization and complete elimination from the human family" of the Jew. To preserve the nation during the Depression he urged the inauguration of a Five Year Plan which would have suspended all civil liberties and democratic practices, including the Congress, and the Supreme Court, and would have placed the country under the control of General Douglas Mac Arthur.

Although this never transpired, Mac Arthur who was chief of staff by September 1930 immediately raised his friend, Van Horne Mosley, to the position of chief of staff with the rank Major General.[32]

Enrollment proceeded very quickly. Menasha's quota of 18 men was rapidly filled. E.P. Mulholland, director of relief work, asserted that they could easily have enrolled twice as many. Some, he claimed, were even "high school graduates." The first complement were sent to Fort Sheridan, Illinois.[33]

By August 1933 the CCC in Wisconsin had 9,400 men dispersed in 47 camps of which 21 were U.S. National Forests, 14 State Forests, and 9 Federal erosion and flood control projects.[34] No camps were established in Winnebago County but men were sent to camps in other parts of Wisconsin and nearby states.

Work in the camps was to be balanced with play. Major General Hugh A. Drum, deputy chief of staff, drafted a recreation program for the CCC. Baseball headed the list of sports and swimming was next in line. Indoor recreation included cards, checkers and dominoes. In addition, the government received a number of offers from colleges to provide education. Soon education became an important part of CCC. By 1937 some 1,100 CCC school buildings with libraries exceeding 1,500 volumes dotted the country. The program offered instruction at all levels including basic literacy, elementary, high school and college courses with vocational training. During the duration of CCC more than 90% of the men were participants in some facet of the education program.[35] The program received great support. Colonel McCormick, publisher of the *Chicago Tribune*, and an implacable foe of Roosevelt, gave the CCC his support. A Chicago judge thought the CCC was largely responsible for a 55% reduction in crime by young men of that day.

To most recruits the CCC was a godsend. Robert Judes, 18, from Oshkosh, who was sent to camps near Crandon, was one of them. He enjoyed the experience. "You were expected to do your work but not kill yourself doing it. We weren't pushed too hard," he admitted. After work there was no lack of entertainment in the area, he went on. "A truck would bring us to town to go to a movie or some other thing--it was usually other things, like ogling girls on the street." Another enlistee, Jack Driscoll, 23, of Neenah, worked in a camp at Conover, near Eagle River. He said the food was good and schooling was also offered. "Most of them kids were better off when they left than when they came it," he claimed. "They had learned a lot." Driscoll suggested that the biggest accomplishment of the CCC was cleaning lakes and streams. "We cleaned all the debris out, stocked them with fish and sank brush racks."[36]

But by no means did the CCC appeal to all recruits. The disciplined life led to many defections. Complaints about food and accommodations could result in dishonorable discharges. Nonetheless, most judged the CCC a great success story.

The impact of monthly $25 allotment checks to families was felt in the economy in cities and towns all across the country. More than $72 million in allotments was making life a little easier at home. In communities close to the camps, local purchases averaging about $5,000 monthly, staved off failure for many small businesses. By 1935, individual congressmen and senators were quick to realize the importance of the camps to their constituencies and political futures. Soon letters and telegrams flooded Fechner's office, most of them demanding new camps in their states. By the end of 1935 there were over 2,650 camps in operation in all states. Nevertheless, as of December 1941, 413,600 CCC men deserted (almost 14% of the total). Another 209,496 (about 7%) were discharged for disciplinary reasons.

Determining the overall success of the CCC in Wisconsin is not clear cut. On one hand, it put about 14,500 men in a work program in any given year from its inception to its dismantlement. But as unemployment in Wisconsin ranged from 200,000 in 1933 to 118,000 in 1935 the CCC was only a small answer to an immense problem. In any case, it kept thousands of young men in time-consuming work and prevented the further swelling of relief rolls.[37]

1933 not only saw the increased role of the federal government in the lives of American citizens but the end of the Prohibition experiment. A chorus of voices pointed out that abolition of the so-called "Great Experiment" would mean thousands of jobs in the production of beer and liquor would be restored. It was a potent argument when so many were out of work.

The problem of drinking had begun in the colonies. When the *Arabella* arrived in 1630 with the main contingent of settlers for Massachusetts it carried 10,000 gallons of beer and 120 hogsheads of malt for brewing more.[38] Drinking soon spread over the eastern seaboard. Peter Stuyvesant, the governor of New

Amsterdam from 1647 to 1664, noted that one quarter of the houses in town were devoted to the sale of brandy, tobacco and beer.[39]

Attempts at prohibition came early. In 1735, for example, a law prohibited the importation of hard liquor to Georgia but it was repealed eight years later when it was learned that local farmers were abandoning their crops to concentrate on making liquor illegally.[40] Drinking continued apace and some historians estimate that by 1810 over twenty-five million gallons of liquor were produced in commercial distilleries and eight million gallons more were imported. These figures do not include beer, wine and cider, not generally conceived of then as intoxicating. As there were only three million male and female whites in the county over fifteen years of age, it was a prodigious amount of consumption. By the early nineteenth century America was on the way of becoming an alcohol-soaked nation, the consequences of which, as many reformers pointed out, were broken lives and families.[41]

Attempts at reform continued. In 1851 prohibitionists in the new state of Wisconsin forced a referendum on the issue and narrowly won, 27,519 to 24,109. But the legislature declined to go along and liquor remained legal.[42] The reformers did not shrink. Although it took half a century, they finally founded the Wisconsin Anti-Saloon League in 1898 with headquarters in Milwaukee. The reformers had a real fight on their hands; not only were thirteen of the forty-six members of the city council saloon keepers but as well they faced the enormous power of the Wisconsin Brewers' Association.[43] Nevertheless, public reaction against the liquor trade continued. It was ably assisted by important clergymen such as the Reverend Mark Mathews, Moderator of the Presbyterian General Assembly, who in 1912 called the liquor traffic, "the most fiendish, corrupt and hell-soaked institution that ever crawled out of the slime of the eternal pit."[44]

By Mathews' day, the tide was flowing strongly in the direction of reform. Before World War I more than two-thirds of the states were dry. The war also aided the movement. Grain used for the production of liquor was now needed to feed the army and American allies. In Neenah the League distributed leaflets in the local schools documenting how wasteful practices of the brewers were directly impeding the war effort on the home front. The League calculated that three million tons of coal were being used to haul grain and fuel the breweries, while an additional six million tons went into the manufacture of beer. It asked plaintively: "Shall we give up everything but booze to win the war?"

But most effective was the League's relentless assault on the Germans engaged in the beer industry and thought to be disloyal. No longer beer, but "Kaiser-brew" became the object of the Anti-Saloon League's invective. Always quick with alliterative phrase and metaphor, the League depicted pro-German utterances as the "froth of the German beer saloon." The bar rail was the altar of sedition, the bartender the high priest dispensing the sacrament of discontent and dissension.[45]

The Anti-Prohibitionists fought back, but their counterattacks proved futile. The tide for prohibition was too strong to stem. On January 16, 1919 the Eighteenth Amendment became a part of the Constitution of the United States. According to its terms, the manufacture, sale and transportation of intoxicating liquors was to be prohibited exactly one year later. The amendment was formally added to the Constitution in June 1920.[46]

To enforce the amendment Congressman Andrew J. Volkstead of Minnesota introduced a bill to define as intoxicating any liquor containing 0.5% alcohol. This was, however, not new as it already existed in many state prohibition laws. The House on that same day by a vote of 176 to 55 passed it. After some difficulty the bill finally became law on October 28, 1919.[47]

Some minor concessions to drinkers were made. In the privacy of their homes people could serve any intoxicating liquids prior to the passage of the Volkstead Act. Moreover, people could make cider, fruit juices and other drinks for use in their own homes. These beverages were considered intoxicating only if a jury in each case determined that they were indeed intoxicating, irrespective of their actual alcoholic content. Finally, the Volkstead Act permitted the sale of alcohol for medical, sacramental and industrial purposes.[48]

Prohibition dealt Wisconsin a heavy blow. Almost 10,000 saloons and 137 breweries closed. Moreover, it was difficult to enforce. Most people in Winnebago County drank as it part of their daily lives and they thought of it as a basic right.[49] As a consequence, the law was often broken. People secretly made and sold liquor. When they delivered to customers they hid small bottles in their boots and were thusly called *bootleggers*. Special saloons to sell the home brew were opened and were called *speakeasies* because only customers who whispered the identifying password could get in. In addition beer flats abounded. These were single family homes in which a room was set aside for the purposes of selling beer, moonshine and playing cards.[50] So much booze was produced that city sewers in Oshkosh were often clogged because home-brewers dumped their mash down the drain. Indeed, in Oshkosh's Sixth Ward fermenting hops could be smelled on any street. Police did very little to stop it because they often drank themselves.[51]

The making of hard liquor, popularly known as *moonshine*, soon became a cottage industry.

> It did not require much equipment; all that was needed was a copper wash boiler, some copper tubing, a 50-gallon garbage can, and a wooden barrel that had a charcoal-lined interior. Ingredients were about 50 pounds of sugar, one-half bushel of cracked corn, a little yeast and some warm water. The fluid from this mash would be placed in a still and the resulting vapors condensed into alcohol, usually 100 proof. The resulting liquid was aged in a barrel, the longer the better. It was then bottled in ½ pint or 1 pint or in gallon jars. Prices varied depending upon supply and demand. One dollar a pint was considered a very good price.[52]

By no means was the selling of beer and liquor without its perils. Wisconsin had a commissioner who enforced prohibition. In 1922 alone 4,000 people were found guilty of such crimes and $509,000 in fines were collected. Even so many complaints continued to arise from the sale of illegal liquor that Congress passed the Jones Law, named after Senator Wesley C. Jones, which amended the Volkstead Act by raising the maximum penalties for first offenses, initially six months in jail or a fine of $1,000 to five years or $10,000 or both. The law went into effect in March 1929. Under the new statute anyone who bought a bottle, a drink--or who had seen a *bootlegger* or *speakeasy* in operation--could be charged with a felony if he failed to disclose what he knew to federal authorities. The protest which followed was immediate, national, bitter and abusive. The law was said to be a vindictive and a sinister move against anyone who in any way opposed Prohibition.[53] Under the Jones Law, Prohibition reached its apex; thereafter, its potency began a precipitous decline. The Depression, itself, dealt it a fatal blow.

In February 1933 Congress adopted a resolution proposing the Twenty-First Amendment to the Constitution to repeal the Eighteenth. The amendment had to be approved by a majority of states. Of these, Michigan was the first and Wisconsin the second. On December 5, 1933 Utah became the thirty-sixth to ratify the amendment and repeal was achieved. After repeal a few states continued statewide prohibition but by 1966 all had abandoned it.[54]

The repeal of Prohibition and the return of Gambrinus' foamy elixir was widely celebrated in the cities of Winnebago County. Huge crowds clustered in whatever drinking establishment they could find to savor their first legal drink in over a decade. In a small way the resumption of brewing had an ameliorative effect on the local economy. The Oshkosh Brewing Company, the largest of several county breweries, which had limped through the Prohibition years by producing syrup, near-beer, and soft drinks, was now in a position to hire a couple hundred new employees. Nonetheless, such benefits were but a proverbial "drop in the ocean," as the employment picture reached its nadir in the bleak winter of 1932-33.[55]

As virtually every economic indicator would suggest, Winnebago County went through its greatest trial during the year 1933. Nowhere was the burden greater than in the city of Oshkosh. Neenah and Menasha, heavily reliant upon paper mills and foundries, suffered as well but neither as long or to the same extent as Oshkosh. Neenah industries had not experienced the immediate impact of the crash of 1929. As late as the end of 1930, it was reported that plants and mills were still operating at full or part-time capacity and there was no laying off of skilled workers nor were there any significant wage reductions.[56] Paper products seemed more resistant to hard times than woodworking mills and allied automotive plants. When the New Deal programs emerged in 1933 the Federal government actually awarded contracts to paper mills to produce the paper which would come cascading out of newly created Federal agencies. Oshkosh, on the other hand, felt the impact of the crash in a more immediate way. The home construction boom of the Twenties trailed off so significantly in the Thirties that the market for sashes and doors--still a significant portion of the city's industrial establishment--evaporated in a flash. It is estimated that in 1930 that one in five Oshkosh workers were without employment. By 1933 only one in three was consistently at work.[57]

Bank clearings, a measure of the volume of trade passing through a community, fell in Oshkosh from $49.6 million to just $20 million in 1933. With depositors reaching into their savings, provided their banks were still viable operations, meant that bank deposits which had reached $17.4 million in 1929 were reduced to $11 million in 1933. In Oshkosh itself construction work had fallen from over $2.7 million in 1926 to just $262,000 in 1933. Moreover, the median weekly wage had fallen to $10.00 in 1933, only a dollar or two more than it was back in the strike year of 1898.[58]

The Paine Lumber Company's experience was typical of the plight of Oshkosh's other woodworking mills when the Depression set in. On the eve of the crash, the company had celebrated its peak production years in 1927 through 1928. In 1929 it employed upwards of 2,000 employees, making it hands-down the largest employer in the county. Its plant was a sprawling behemoth, stretching for sixty acres along the Fox River, on what is now both sides of Congress Avenue. By late 1932 Paine was the only mill still running regularly, but was doing so, well below capacity and with a workforce that would have to be described as skeletal. It is estimated that the company laid off nearly 1600 workers between 1930 and 1933.

But the Paine Lumber Company was not just one of the run-of-the-mill mills. Along with the Morgan Company it had roots reaching back to the origins of the city. In the late nineteenth-century it hired hundreds of immigrants, many of them young children from Germany and Poland who lived and worked under hazardous conditions with extraordinarily low pay. The Paine family philosophy had always been to treat labor just like any other commodity: get it as cheaply as possible. In 1898, although several other mills resisted striker demands for higher wages, it was the Paine Company that led the resistance to labor demands. Under the leadership of Charles Paine, the owners prevailed upon the governor to send the state militia to wear down the strikers and protect strikebreakers. Memories of these unsavory days, only three decades old, lingered among Oshkosh's working classes in the Thirties.[59]

In 1927, the new president of the Paine Lumber Company, Nathan Paine, made the somewhat questionable decision to build a new home for him and his wife, Jessie Kimberly, a member of the famous paper making family of Neenah. Designed by local architect Bryan Fleming in the Tudor Revival style, it was situated on the northeast corner of Algoma Boulevard and Congress Street, practically in sight of the very humble tenements the Paines had built for some of their poorest paid workers. Construction costs alone were astronomical, topping off at about $300,000. By contrast, the average working class home in Oshkosh at the time ranged between three and seven-thousand dollars. Workers and passersby observed crate after crate of fine furnishings, acquisitions and European paintings being loaded into the house as it neared completion.

Work continued in the interior of the house even as the Depression worsened, although the Paines did postpone their art-buying spree and even began to liquidate it. Nonetheless, to the workingmen of Oshkosh the palatial mansion struck them as the flaunting of opulence during a time of wholesale despair. Workers, it is said, left notes for the Paines declaring they would blow the place up if the family every attempted to move into it. Not only had so many lost their jobs with the company, former employees were shocked when the Paine Thrift Bank, an institution in which workers had been cajoled and enticed by the company to place their meager savings, abruptly closed in early 1933. Insult was added to injury when the former depositors were informed they were being held responsible for the bank's deficits. One child of the Depression remembered how indignant his father had been at the obvious extravagance of the Paines. "What a waste!" he intoned, "they gallivanting around Europe on a shopping spree after their bank failed. How the Paines ever thought they could come back to Oshkosh is beyond me."[60]

Hard times even afflicted other wealthy families in Oshkosh. William Radford, the young scion to the Radford Company woodworking fortune, recalled the family's wonderfully enormous home on Algoma Street, noting that "it was quite a neighborhood." When the Depression caught up with the Radfords they were obliged to give up the big house. "We made less money," William laconically observed, "and moved to Park Street." Apparently unaffected by the low prices for milk, the Carver family, which operated the city's largest dairy and creamery, and who resided in a comfortable home on Merritt Street, did reasonably well during the Depression. As Hugh Carver, a young man of the time, recalled, "[We] were in the food business and people had to eat." But even those who were not scarred by destitution had to be sensitive to the plight of those less fortunate. Young Hugh remembered using the family car to date a girl who lived on 11th Street on the city's working class South side. When he dropped his date off at the end of one evening, the girl's father came out and vented his spleen upon poor Hugh. "You northsiders," he bellowed, "think you're so hot, taking these girls out."[61]

As 1933 drew to a close the perennially sanguine *Oshkosh Northwestern* bid farewell to the old year and peered with "confident hope" into the new one. The editor trusted that the next twelve months would become the "dividing line marking the end of four years of the most severe economic depression," and anchored this optimism in "abundant evidences...that point the way to better times in the coming year than at any period since 1929." This end-of-year editorial was buttressed by a second one with the banner headline: Outlook for 1934 is Bright! "The path to economic recovery appears to have fewer steep grades and rocks of obstruction and pessimism," it claimed, and while there might be " considerable hard going in places...the bumps and chuck-holes are being ironed out and progress ought to be fairly rapid and certain...and we can hail 1934 with revived courage and hopefulness."[62]

If the *Oshkosh Northwestern's* forecast smacked of too much wishful-thinking and local "boosterism," at least it was supported by local manufacturers and business leaders. They, too, looked to real recovery in the new year 1934. During recent years, most manufacturers had merely "hoped" for economic revival. On the eve of 1934, they claimed they could "feel" economic improvement. Again, certain signs pointed in this direction. Many business leaders looked to the economic spark being provided by the recently inaugurated Civil Works Projects which was creating jobs (however temporarily), improving civilian morale, and increased consumer buying power. These and other signs presaged better times in 1934, or so it was thought.[63]

Notes

1. *WLMR*, February 1933, No. 2, p. 4.
2. Donald C. Leach, *Good Riddance to Bad Rubbish: First 100 Years of the Leach Company*. (Oshkosh: Leach Company, 1987), p. 73.
3. Winnebago County Clerk. *Proceedings of the Board of Supervisors*. Vol. 17, November 1932 to March 1936. Resolution No. 73, November 29, 1932, p. 74.
4. *MR*, December 30, 1932.
5. *Oshkosh Northwestern*, January 4, 1933.
6. *MR*, February 7, 1933.
7. *WBB* 1933, pp. 114-15.
8. A. William Hoglund, "Wisconsin Dairy Farmers on Strike," *Agricultural History*, Vol. 35, (January 1961), p. 24.
9. *WB 1933*, pp. 132, 133, 139.
10. Herbert Jacobs, "The Wisconsin Milk Strikes," *Wisc Magazine of History*. (Autumn, 1951), Vol. 35, No. 1, p. 31.
11. Hoglund, "Wisconsin Dairy Farmers on Strike", p. 24.
12. *MR*, February 15, 1933.
13. *MR*, February 21, 1933.
14. *Oshkosh Northwestern*, February 22, 1933.
15. *MR*, February21, 1933.
16. *MR*, February 23, 1933; *Oshkosh Northwestern*, May 17, 1933. See also, SHSW, Mss. 26, Wisconsin Cooperative Milk Pool Records, 1932-1943, Box 1 Committee Minutes. Folder: Minutes Board, 1933-1940.
17. *MR*, March 9, 1933.
18. *Oshkosh Northwestern*, January 25, 1933.
19. *MR*, March 3, 1933.
20. Edwin Hill, *In the Shadow of the Mountain: The Spirit of the CCC*, pp. xii-xiv.
21. Glad, *War, a New Era, and Depression*, p. 357.
22. *MR*, March 6, 1933.
23. *MR*, March 15, 1933.
24. *MR*, March 15, 1933.
25. S.F. Shattuck, *A History of Neenah*. (Neenah: Private Publisher, 1958), pp. 110-11;

Michael J. Goc, *Winneconne: History's Crossing Place*. (Friendship, WI: New Past Press, Inc., 1987), pp. 75-76.
26. *MR*, March 8, 1933.
27. *WWB, 1933*, pp. 71-72.
28. John A. Salmond, *The Civilian Conservation Corps, 1933-1942: A New Deal Case Study*. (Durham, NC: Duke University Press, 1967), p. 31. The CCC lasted until June 30, 1942 when it was abolished by Congress.
29. Salmond, *The Civilian Conservation Corps*, pp. 36-37. In May 1933 the Corps was authorized to enroll 25,000 war veterans with no age or marital limitations imposed.
30. *The Code of the Laws of the United States of America of a General and Permanent Character in Force January 3, 1935*. 1934 edition (Washington, D.C.: U.S. Government Printing Office, 1935), p. 673.
31. Salmond, *The Civilian Conservation Corps*, p. 33. The United States was divided into nine army corps areas. Wisconsin, along with Illinois and Michigan formed the Sixth Corps who commander was Major General Frank R. McCoy. He established his headquarters in the Post Office Building, Chicago. See Alison Otis, William Honey, et al. *The Forest Service and the Civilian Conservation Corps, 1933-1942*. (Washington: U.S. Department of Agriculture Forest Service, August 1986), p. 11.
32. James F. & Jean H. Vivian, "The Bonus March of 1932: The Role of General George Van Horne Mosely," *Wisc. Magazine of History*. Vo. 51, No. 1 (Autumn 1967), p. 30.
33. *MR*, April 24 and April 26, 1933.
34. Otis, Honey et al., *The Forest Service and the Civilian Conservation Corps*, p. 11
35. Otis, Honey et al., *The Forest Service and the Civilian Conservation Corps*, p. 11.
36. *Oshkosh Northwestern*, August 15, 1991.
37. Raymond E. Porter, *A Survey and Analysis of Works Progress Administration and Public Works Administrations Undertakings in the State of Wisconsin, 1933-1939*. Master of Science Thesis, University of Wisconsin, 1950, p. 2.
38. Jack S. Blocker, Jr., *The American Temperance Movements: Cycle of Reform*. (Boston: Twayne Publishers, 1989), p. 3.
39. Edward Behr, *Prohibition: Thirteen Years That Changed America*. (NY: Arcade Publishing, 1996), p. 9.
40. Blocker, *The American Temperance Movement*, p. 6.
41. Norman H. Clark, *Deliver Us from Evil: An Interpretation of the American Prohibition*. (NY: W.W. Norton & Col., Inc., 1976), p. 19.
42. Dennis McCann, *The Wisconsin Story: 150 Stories, 150 Years*. (Milwaukee: Milwaukee Journal-Sentinel, n.d.), p. 11.
43. Jeffrey Lucker, *The Politics of Prohibition in Wisconsin, 1917-1933*. MA Thesis, University of Wisconsin, 1968, pp. 2-3.
44. Clark, *Deliver Us from Evil*, p. 4.
45. Lucker, *The Politics of Prohibition in Wisconsin*, pp. 111-12.
46. Paul Glad, "John Barleycorn," *Wisconsin Magazine of History*. Vol. 68 (Winter 1984-85), p. 119.
47. Behr, *Prohibition*, p. 229.
48. Glad, "Barleycorn," p. 131.
49. UWO-ARC, *Oral Interview with Clarence Jungwirth*, October 1994.
50. UWO-ARC, *Oral Interview with Mr. Pierce*, January 31, 1995.

51. UWO-ARC, *Oral Interview with Eugene Steckbauer,* October 21, 1995.
52. Clarence Jungwirth, *History of the Bloody Sixth Ward in Oshkosh.* (Oshkosh: Self-Published, n.d.), p. 59.
53. Clark, *Deliver Us from Evil,* p. 193.
54. *New Encyclopedia Britannica,* Vol. 9 (1991), p. 174.
55. Steve R. Langkau, *A Thumbnail History of Former City of Oshkosh Industrial Firms.* (Oshkosh: Private Publisher, 2004), p. 71.
56. *Neenah Daily News Times,* November 10, 1930.
57. James I. Metz, *Foundations to Remember: Reflections upon Oshkosh's 150 Years.* (Oshkosh: Polemics Press, 2003), p. 29.
58. Michael C. Goc, *Oshkosh: 150 Years,* pp. 169-70.
59. For a history of the 1898 woodworkers' strike see Virginia Crane, *The Oshkosh Woodworkers' Strike of 1898: A Wisconsin Community in Crisis.* (Oshkosh: V. Crane, 1998).
60. John Livingstone, *The Importance of Being from Oshkosh: Looking Back at the Great Depression, World War II and the Cold War Years.* (Pacific Grove, CA: Park Place Productions, 2002), pp. 44-46.
61. Michael Goc, *Oshkosh at 150,* p. 44.
62. *Oshkosh Northwestern,* December 30, 1933.
63. "1934 Outlook Brighter Say Local Firms," *Oshkosh Northwestern,* Dec. 30, 1933.

Chapter 6

1934: New Directions in Relief

A serious problem facing the new administration throughout 1933 was the impending collapse of the public welfare programs in the various states, and the counties, cities and towns within them. The jurisdictions within Winnebago County had already critically strained their resources by this time. For example, in Menasha, Mayor N.G. Remmel in March told the city council that the budget for poor relief and unemployment work would be exhausted within sixty days.[1] In Neenah, Mayor George Sande stated that as all other relief projects had been exhausted, he proposed to the council the establishment of a municipal garden project that would buy 85 acres for $2,000. More than fifty men a day would be given work cultivating garden plots to provide food for themselves for the winter months. The council agreed.[2] And in Oshkosh, where unemployment and relief demands were the greatest in the county, the question of what to do became a volatile topic.

In what was known as the "First 100 Days," Congress, under President Roosevelt's prodding, elected to assume an expanded role in mitigating the distress plaguing the nation. On May 12, 1933 Congress created the Federal Emergency Relief Administration (FERA). The new agency received $500 million for distribution to the states, half that sum was for matching grants with the states contributing three dollars for every one they received in federal assistance. The other half was to form a discretionary fund from which sums could be granted to those states where relief needs were so pressing that they could not meet the matching provisions. Moreover, the act was intended as well to render services, materials and/or commodities to provide the necessities of life to persons in dire need.

Harry Hopkins, Roosevelt's appointed head of FERA, took office on May 22, 1933 and approved the first grants the following day. Between late May and the end of December 1933, FERA allocated over $324 million to the 48 states and all territories. By March 1934 nearly 3,700,00 families and single persons were receiving relief; one month later the figure escalated to 4,500,000. All this called for an expansion of staff throughout the country.[3] The states spent FERA funds on both work relief and direct relief. Initially, they paid for work performed through a voucher system rather than cash; however, after March 1934 all work was paid for with wages, even though direct relief most often came in the form of grocery orders; or most unsatisfactory of all, orders on commissaries or central warehouses.[4]

FERA proved the effectiveness of the granted aid system, providing an attractive incentive that the states found irresistible. Even though states like Wisconsin had clamored for federal aid because they claimed to be stretched beyond all means, they invariably found money to match the new federal grants.[5] As part of the National Industrial Recovery Act (NIRA) the federal government created the Public Works Administration (PWA) in June 1933. In practice the PWA did no construction itself, it loaned money to state and local governments and to locally contracted firms. The program as envisioned by its director, Harold Ickes, looked for work programs that could be implemented judiciously and which would last for the long term. Moreover, Ickes did not make as one of the conditions for employment that you were on the relief rolls. PWA moved slowly; it did not increase employment rapidly, indeed, contractors not required to use workers on relief seldom did so.[6]

To supplement FERA's inadequate work relief programs, alleviate suffering, and forestall the impending disaster for the winter of 1933-1934, the national government launched the Civil Works Administration (CWA) in November 1933. Implemented as a stop-gap measure, the CWA was designed to blunt the misery predicted for the looming cold weather winter months. By January 1934, CWA employed 4 million people. The CWA was not relief or a dole. Rather, it put unemployed persons receiving relief back to work. Unlike FERA, CWA paid its workers wages negotiated by PWA in collective bargaining agreements. It pumped $1 billion into the stagnant economy. Half of the CWA workers came from the emergency relief rolls of FERA and the states, and the rest came from the ranks of people who lacked employment and were likely candidates for relief measures. At its peak in January 1934, CWA employed over 4 million workers nationwide. In February, FERA, CCC, and CWA assisted about 8 million households with 28 million people or 22.2% of the American population.[7]

Franklin Roosevelt had always thought of both FERA and CWA as temporary responses to extraordinary crises and not permanent solutions to the languishing economy. When CWA ended in the spring of 1934, its workers were dropped or transferred to FERA. Within a month of the decision to close down CWA, Congress passed the Emergency Relief Appropriations Act, which effectively terminated FERA as well. Critics who predicted hardship when FERA ended were right. The period of transition between FERA and its eventual successor was a time of confusion and near chaos in the history of public relief.[8]

As jobs, not the dole, became the keystone of federal aid, Congress approved the creation of the Works Progress Administration (WPA) in 1935. A few years later, this program's name was changed to the more memorable, Works Projects Administration. Within a year, it employed more than 3 million people and would become the mainstay work relief operation for the remainder of the Depression. WPA decentralized its operation; most WPA undertakings were planned and sponsored by state and local units with 95% of all money going to the latter. WPA drew up elaborate schemes of differential payments called "security wages." They were pegged between wages in the private sector and relief. It was a way of encouraging workers to remain on public projects.

Most of the labor force was unskilled or semi-skilled and the plurality of WPA funds, 38.9%, were spent on the construction or renovation of highways, roads, streets and bridges. Between 1935 and 1942 WPA spent over $15 billion. The largest number of people employed at any one time was 3 million and its rolls never dropped below 1.4 million. Congress would slash the WPA budget nearly in half in 1937 when economic conditions appeared to improve a little. Although funds were raised slightly during the next year during renewed depression, they were cut sharper when Congress ordered everyone employed for 18 months or greater be fired. Congress intended to force project workers to seek private employment.[9]

FERA established rules mandating the ways in which money could be spent. Field agents, each assigned to a group of states, represented the federal administration in contacts with state administrations and interpreted federal policies to state officials. In turn state official explained state policies to federal agents and supervised local efforts. Roosevelt appointed one of his advisors, Harry L. Hopkins (1890-1946) as administrator of FERA at a salary of $10 thousand plus expenses. Hopkins, an Iowa native, had graduated from Grinnell College. Immediately after graduation he went to New York City where he became involved in social work. In 1931 he became chairman of the New York State Temporary Emergency Relief Administration under then Governor Roosevelt.

Despite the rising need for relief, the municipalities of Winnebago County had proven resistant to accepting federal assistance in the early years of the Depression. Even when other cities in Wisconsin bowed to the inevitable, places like Neenah, Menasha and Oshkosh preferred handling the matter on their own. Part of reason that the twin paper mill cities declined federal assistance is that relief needs, though substantial, were not acute enough while employment at the mills remained constant if not irregular from time to time. According to Finley F. Martin, a personnel supervisor at Kimberly-Clark, "[the] paper industry...was one of the least affected industries." Martin ascribed this phenomenon to the theory that "whether industry was expanding or declining paper work was still necessary." After all, he pointed out, "newspapers were published in all that time...there was as much demand for paper (or) almost as much...so the area was quite stable, comfortably stable." Perhaps no one was getting a raise at this time, Martin conceded, "but everything else was dirt cheap too."[10]

Oshkosh's hesitation to embrace federal aid was somewhat more complex. As has already been established, her industries were not depression-proof and unemployment and relief demands rose quickly and dramatically after the onset of the economic crisis. Some have suggested that Winnebago County's inherent conservatism made it distasteful to embrace outside help. Certainly Mayor Taylor Brown's administration was of this persuasion. To the finance committee of the United States Senate, Brown stated that poor relief was "not necessary for Oshkosh as our bonded indebtedness is less than one half the legal limit." And, he added, perhaps pompously, "we can take care of our own." In a final bluster, Brown conceded, while ignoring the proverbial elephant in his own jurisdiction, "some cities that are in poor financial shape will probably need federal or state aid." Brown believed, at least up to the closing months of his administration, that as long as Oshkosh could borrow money or bond itself, it should do so, and pay off the debt burden through tax assessments in future years, rather than accept aid from the federal government. Of course, once federal aid was accepted on a substantial level control over debt relief would pass out of the hands of local appointees and into the hands of state and federal oversight. Nevertheless, even before Brown left office in the spring of 1933 the city was receiving increased levels of federal assistance. The staggering relief needs of the year 1933 would compel the city of Oshkosh and other county municipalities to throw their lot in with the Federal government.[11]

The gradual move towards relying upon federal relief can be charted in innumerable letters and memoranda exchanged between the cities and villages of Winnebago County and state officials in Madison. There were myriad difficulties besetting various municipalities that prompted the adoption of the "county system" of relief that would allow federal dollars to roll into Winnebago County by 1934. The principal reason, as seen in the case of Neenah and Menasha, was the mere exhaustion of city funds to address the relief burden, one that was expected to get worse before it got better. But this was by no means the only issue. In some cases, smaller townships within the county, believed their relief needs were not being addressed fairly. And in the case of Oshkosh, city-mandated salary reductions for relief workers ran afoul of regulations required by the Industrial Commission of the Wisconsin Emergency Relief Agency (WERA).

Despite Mayor Brown's intransigence over the transfer of primary responsibility for relief from the city to the state government, the realities of poor relief in Oshkosh beckoned otherwise. In an Industrial Commission field report in August 1932, Florence Peterson pointed to the "very bleak" employment situation. She reported that factories in Oshkosh were only running a few days a week. Diamond Match Company, which had been doing well was now running flat. The Paine Lumber Company was practically shut down. So, too, was the Morgan Lumber Company. And grass rug companies were also running far below capacity. The only bright spot, according to Peterson, was that Universal was making lighting units and had "picked up a bit and added men." Relief cases had reached an all-time high, topping off at over 1,000. With the approaching change of season, Peterson's alarm was seconded by Edna Roddis, secretary of the Bureau of Family Services, who was convinced that the need to "build up and maintain the morale of the community" were just as important as providing material assistance. From her perspective the ongoing depression had been very hard on families, and the whole structure of family life "may be permanently warped unless they can be helped to make some adjustment."[12]

Referring, no doubt, to an added burden facing Neenah and Menasha in managing their relief responsibilities, L. J. Howman, Superintendent of Outdoor Relief for Winnebago County, reported that because of our "splendid railroad facilities and the reputation of the Fox River Valley as an industrial center, we are blessed with an unusual number of transients." Clarifying that he was not alluding to the "regulation hobo but to those who come here seeking work," he pointed out that the two cities were getting burdened with things like medical bills and funeral expenses that were over-taxing the poor relief budget. Even though transient homes had been established in Green Bay and Oshkosh, the men "do not all take advantage of this arrangement." Ms. Peterson's reply was that once these cities accepted the "county system" of relief they could expect help in this matter.[13]

The allusion to the proper responsibility of other jurisdictions, and belief that their own localities might be getting short-changed in relief dollars, was another reason for the transfer of relief to the county system. Henry Young, a member of the relief committee could commiserate with Oshkosh's problems but opined that "Oshkosh's situation of unemployment was more unusual than elsewhere, because of the woodworking industry, which is operating 15% of normal." Optimistic that recovery would come to the mills of Oshkosh, albeit slower than in other industries, he remained adamant that "Oshkosh's plight should not be divided among others to hold them down, too." The town of Oshkosh was also displeased with its slice of the relief pie as it was being distributed. The town's chairman, C. O. Allen, complained that he was responsible for administering relief to areas like Algoma Park and Nordheim, which according to him, had "filled up with poor folk since the Depression set in" and featured homes no better than "shacks and shanties." He recommended that the town of Oshkosh was "entitled to more of the per capita relief help" than it was presently receiving.[14]

Claims of mismanagement, incompetence, insensitivity to the plight of the poor and the arrogance of certain relief agents lent itself to a general consensus that the local system of administering poor relief was ineffective and that the county system was preferable. Field reports on Oshkosh's poor relief director, Frank Janda, pointed out that while he was a tireless worker and well-disposed to the concerns of his constituents, he was, nonetheless, in over his head. Florence Peterson, once an admirer of Janda, berated the handling of poor relief in the city of Oshkosh, observing that the "entire set-up of relief ... is a most deplorable one." Chief among her complaints was that there was too much friction between city and private relief agencies. She also charged that the city was not hiring trained investigators, so that "cases are therefore inadequately investigated." Finally as she discovered in all the Winnebago jurisdictions, the system of keeping records was abysmal. She yearned for the day when the state and federal government would assume oversight.[15]

Peterson's indictment of the poor relief system in Menasha was even less flattering than that of Oshkosh's. There, according to her field report, John Sensenbrenner was the poor commissioner whom she derided, rather ungenerously, as "fat, ignorant, and wholly unqualified." She painted a portrait of a pathetic figure in Sensenbrenner, a man who was afraid he might lose his job and who claimed that "he would be on the poor list if he didn't get fifty-dollars a month." Sensenbrenner had no assistance, no office, no car and was handling upwards of 140 relief cases. Aware of a movement afoot to remove him from office, Sensenbrenner, according to Peterson's report, "was afraid to ask for help, fearing he will lose his job."[16]

The village of Omro on the western edge of Winnebago County was also finding it difficult to get a handle on poor relief. According to a field report filed by the Industrial Commission and conducted by a Ms. Dresden, the village featured a "good many deserted homes...and there are a good many small shacks," all of which had been filled by squatters. The Marshal of the village administered poor relief, and while he was a "man of great common sense with a humane attitude," according to Dresden, he was totally untrained and a poor record-keeper. Like elsewhere in the county, Dresden asserted that "there is absolutely no planning for the future and for rehabilitation--no records, no centralized planning of any kind." Not only was the village incognizant of how much would be needed in the following year, it had no idea as to where the funding would come.[17]

Nowhere in Winnebago County was relief administered by personal fiat as it was in the case of the Town of Oshkosh. There, C.O. Allen was virtual law unto himself. A pig farmer and town chairman, Allen came from a large family with many political connections; in fact, his brother Dave had been the former District Attorney for the county. Ms. Dresden was apparently not impressed in her meeting with Allen, describing him as a "very arrogant, hot-headed man...with a great sense of his own importance and the members of his family." By his own admission, Allen presided over considerable relief concerns, particularly in the West Algoma and Nordheim districts which he described as slums. He dispensed charity as if the town was his own fiefdom. Applicants for aid were compelled to show up at Allen's own home, where they would be given vouchers or order books to turn over to the local grocer. Attached to the order book were a list of rules and regulations for those accepting relief, the contents of which can only be characterized as draconian in nature.

It was a bit of a conundrum having Allen dispense poor relief. Personally, he did not believe that "there was a necessity for relief," save for old age and serious illnesses. Convinced that most of his constituents had "wasted their money in riotous living when wages were high," he alleged that most of them had automobiles but "no cows." In conversations with Mr. Janda and the county nurse, Dresden learned that Allen was "one of the most disagreeable men in the county with whom to talk." It was common knowledge that he yelled and hollered at all of the families who were forced to seek his assistance and that many of the strictly unemployed would not apply to him for relief, preferring "to suffer rather than be so treated." Dresden concluded her characterization of Allen by charging that "he has no consideration and dispenses relief with a high hand."[18]

It is little wonder, then, that as the cities and townships of Winnebago County approached the matter of poor relief for fiscal year 1934 that they were prepared to forego local administration in favor of the county system. Several jurisdictions were relieved to hand over the problem to the county, state and federal government. Only the city of Oshkosh proved resistant to change. Mayor Oaks and the common council were determined to maintain a controlling influence over the way in which the city managed relief. In the fall of 1933 the city and the Industrial Commission had a running dispute over the city's attempt to reduce the salaries of those in the poor department. Then, it appeared as though the city had capitulated. On October 2 the common council with the mayor's endorsement a week later, resolved it "would cease providing poor relief on the first day of January 1934, and turn such relief over to the County of Winnebago on that date." Yet, on November 2 the Winnebago County Board of Supervisors voted down such a resolution by a 26 to 6 vote. According to the report, the votes in support of defeating the county plan "were mustered entirely from the city of Oshkosh." Such histrionics proved to be the last hurrah of a disgruntled minority. Forced with the forfeit of substantial federal aid, the city of Oshkosh crumbled and embraced the county system by the close of 1933. The entire county went into the new system by the start of 1934.[19]

Given the allusions to transients and hoboes complicating the distribution of poor relief and exacerbating the crisis, a word or two more on crime is necessary. Police reports from the Thirties are irregular at best and the *Uniform Crime Reports*, first published in 1930, only give a breakdown of crimes by state, not by county or municipal jurisdiction. The sensational reports of prohibition violation and the rise of organized crime in major cities would seem to suggest that this was a lawless era. True enough, the cities of Winnebago County recorded substantial numbers of violations of the Volkstead Act, but evidence, mostly anecdotal, does not suggest that personal or property crimes were particularly remarkable during the Thirties within the county. In the improbable case that some of the more notorious bank robbers of the era, like Bonne and Clyde or John Dillinger, who, indeed, had robbed a bank in Racine in 1933, came calling, the colorful Oshkosh Chief of Police, Arthur H. Gabbert, was ready. He equipped one of the city's police department cars with a bullet-proof windshield, and after a Green Bay bank was robbed in the summer of 1931, he purchased a junk car and had it riddled with a machine gun, then parked it in front of city hall as a sober deterrent to aspiring bank robbers.[20]

With the high demands placed upon poor relief needs in the City of Oshkosh, transients were perceived as a serious concern. During its brief tenure, the "Hotel Depression" took measures to encourage those who were "just passing through" did exactly that. All along the rails connecting the Fox Valley, in certain wooded stands and cleared meadows, hobo camps were easily detectable.

One young man during the Depression could recall when disheveled men would come to his back door seeking food or a little cash. If his mother was disposed to give them a handout, they "would show their appreciation by marking with chalk a cross on the sidewalk in front of our house, signifying to their fellow 'knights of the road' that they could expect a soft touch at 177 Central Avenue." On the south side of town, young Clarence Jungwirth could remember the same scene playing itself out.[21]

Hoboes seemed to like concentrating up the line from Oshkosh in the environs of Neenah and Menasha. As early as the end of 1930 the *Daily News Times* reported that the city of Neenah was "being visited by large numbers of the transient unemployed, either passing through or [who] have come here seeking work." According to John Scanlon, a guard for the railroad yard in Neenah, hoboes liked the boxcars there because there was always paper in them that could be arranged into bedding. Acknowledging that most hoboes were simply good men down on their luck, Scanlon recalled many a scrape he had with more truculent tramps. The Neenah yard could be so tough that the police "would stay away...they knew they had problems on their hands the minute they got mixed up with a bunch of hobos." Scanlon observed that the worst period was between 1929 and 1935, just after the crash yet before the arrival of federal work projects. On one evening during this time, Scanlon opened a bunch of empty boxcars only to count some thirty-nine hoboes come tumbling out.[22]

Although the burden of relief being lifted from the shoulders of local municipalities was comforting, the county still looked at the approaching winter of 1933-1934 with a great degree of trepidation. While the paper mills in Neenah and Menasha were still operating at tolerable levels, the woodworking mills in Oshkosh were all but closed. Many were concerned that the degree of relief required to see the winter through would overwhelm even the generous federal assistance about to pour into the county. That is why the citizens of the county were elated with the introduction of CWA projects in November 1933. This optimism, however, was tempered by the experience of a municipal work project undertaken by the City of Oshkosh back in 1931. The brainchild of then Mayor Brown, Councilman Hagene and Commissioner Oaks, the Oshkosh Lakeshore Improvement project was designed to provide jobs at a time when industrial capacity of the city was at 45% of its 1928 level. The project planned was to improve Miller's Bay at Menominee Park. Marshy areas were to be drained and filled in and a breakwater was to be constructed in order to provide a haven for boats. The city anteed up some $96,000 for the project, a considerable sum given the hard times. Commissioner Oaks wanted to get immediately started with the work but was hamstrung by a city law that required contractors to submit competitive bids for any work performed that would cost $500 or more. Dredging and hauling costs would surely far exceed that amount. To get around this obstacle, Oaks hired his own contractors and paid them in installments of $495. In one case, a trucking firm owned by Chris M. Genal, a former saloon keeper from the south side, would receive over time some forty-nine such payments.

There were other contractors who received similar largesse but Genal's operation became the lightning rod of criticism.

Leading opponents of the project belonged to the Oshkosh Better Government League, a group of Oshkosh outsiders who had organized under the rallying cry to bring back to the city the mayor-council form of government. They were convinced that the commission system had grown ineffective, wasteful, and now patently dishonest. In fact, the very creation of the opposition newspaper, the *Fox Valley Square Dealer,* can be traced to the park improvement project. Editor Roland Senn was relentless in haranguing the system and dubbed the project the "495" in his editorials; the name stuck. At one point in one of his editorials, Senn accused Genal of illegally evading the city bidding process. Genal was incensed and decided to get even. He sued Senn and the paper for libel and won the case. This led to the untimely demise of the *Fox Valley Square Dealer.* The opposition cudgel was taken up by the *Fox Valley Free Press* under the more judicious and circumspect pen of Lynn Peavey. The improvements at Menominee Park were completed but no additional work projects were considered and the experience had jaded most of those involved.[23]

Included in the ranks of those wary of work projects were the very ones hired to do the work on Miller Bay. Given the fragile condition of city finances, Oaks had devised a method of paying workers in vouchers redeemable at local Oshkosh businesses. Clarence Jeske, secretary of the "Oshkosh Unemployed Council," and a worker on the site raised objections to this form of reimbursement. Insisting that workers were not slaves, Jeske and his followers demanded cash payment. Frank Janda, a former cigar-maker and local labor leader at the time, and who had served on the executive board of the Wisconsin Federation of Labor in the Twenties, sympathized with the workers but had no authority to initiate changes. On April 30, 1931, Jeske confronted Janda at his city hall office. Jeske and Janda had a heated exchange which included some shouting and the pounding of desks. Jeske was so vituperative and threatening that he had to be arrested.

The following day, May 1, was the traditional European workers holiday and one that was celebrated by socialists and communists worldwide. A crowd of nearly 500 crowded Monument Square and demanded Jeske's release. They also listened to speeches by members of the Unemployed Council and several wild orations by "unnamed persons" identified as communists, largely from Milwaukee. The gathering then sent a delegation to city hall reiterating their demands for Jeske's release and the implementation of cash relief pay at 50 cents per hour. The *Oshkosh Northwestern* rightly dismissed the proceedings as a tempest in a teapot. "The demonstration was not of enough size to cause any apprehension," the paper noted, "and police were on guard to step in if the privilege of free speech should be abused to the extent of inciting riot or spreading incendiarism." The open-air venting did not lead to any riot and Jeske remained incarcerated.[24]

Several weeks later, William Balsey, one of the May Day speakers, asked to reserve space at Menominee Park for four consecutive Thursday evenings to hold open forums for the unemployed. The Park Board, noting the anarchistic and communist tenor of the May Day proceedings, were wary of granting permission. Board member William Maxcy judged that he did not believe "persons should be allowed to attack the government and American institutions." When Balsey could not provide an ironclad guarantee that the character of the speeches would be non-inflammatory, the Board denied the request. Although disgruntled, the workers did not strike the Miller Bay project and accepted the reimbursement arrangement as proscribed.[25]

Notwithstanding this bad experience with subsidized projects, Winnebago County anxiously awaited news of impending assistance from the Federal government at the end of 1933. Under CWA, municipalities could proposed projects that would improve the public domain only. Initially, private projects were approved but when it came to actually funding them the national office declared that such projects were impossible to subsidize. Hence, improvement projects like the one proposed for the Twin Lakes Boy Scout reservation were subsequently denied funding. Municipalities were also responsible for 50% of the funding, all of the materials for any given project, and workers must come from the ranks of those on relief rolls.[26]

Although it preceded the implementation of CWA sponsorship, one project under the direction of the NRA set the general tone for later ones. On October 28, 1933 word was disseminated that a project involving the relocation of Highway 41 south of Oshkosh would be soon underway. It was hoped some 84 men would be hired for the job. The men, it was proposed, would be given thirty hours a week for work with unskilled laborers receiving a flat rate of 55 cents per hour and those with designated skills could make hourly wages between 65 cents and $1.15. Only local contractors were permitted to submit bids and they were expected to use only local men and pay the appropriate scale of wages. On November 1, the contract, totaling $37,373.31 was awarded to J. Rasmussen and Sons.[27]

The formal inauguration of the CWA in Winnebago County occurred when delegates of its cities and townships traveled to Milwaukee on November 12 to submit applications for their share of federal tax dollars. Oshkosh went to Milwaukee with ambitious plans to secure entitlement to $120,000 of the total amount allotted to the state. Oshkosh submitted eight major projects of local improvement with plans to employ 600-700 men. High on the list of priorities was a major overhaul of a local athletic field. Neenah submitted bids on five projects. Four of them dealt with its city's parks, involving seeding grass, removing dead trees and replanting them with new ones and shrubs in Riverside, Lauden, and Kimberly Point, as well as the widening and grading of the parking lot at Riverside Park. Its principal project was the removal of obstacles and debris from the Fox River channel and the removal of sludge deposits from the sewer outlets in the river and lower Lake Butte des Morts. Neenah hoped to acquire $45,000 in order to employ 100 men for six months and 200 for three months. Workers would be paid 40 cents an hour, and it was hoped that would make them self-supporting. Menasha proposed general park land developments, work on a retaining wall along the government canal, and a cleaning of the east shore of lower Lake Butte des Morts.[28]

Most of the projects were approved and work began immediately. Public response was quick and favorable. Most felt that the CWA projects were immeasurably better than the pure dole system. It gainfully employed many throughout the first half of 1934 who had been languishing on the relief rolls for months, which, in turn, provided some relief to local taxpayers. Moreover, good work was being done that otherwise would not have been affordable. Even before 1933 ended, figures from Oshkosh indicated that had the CWA projects not been implemented, there would have been an all time record set for families on the dole. Some 800 families were removed from the relief list during the month of December 1933 as a result of the CWA. Nonetheless, the prospects for 1934, even with the CWA as an offset, did not appear to look any better because of an expected increase in the amount of local unemployment.[29]

Whatever satisfaction was derived from the promising reports of the CWA, was sharply countered by an impending sense of doom. Like the proverbial sword of Damocles, knowledge that the projects were short-lived produced an anxiety that hovered over everyone in the county. As early as January 1934, the national office of the CWA announced that the quota of federal jobs in Wisconsin would be reduced from 160,000 to 100,000. In Winnebago County the enforced reduction of January 15 would mean the loss of CWA employment to 916 persons. This action, though expected in theory, shocked people into reality. Before accepting this step, Wisconsinites attempted to winnow those from the program who might not need help as much as others. Workers who held life insurance policies exceeding $300 and those households with a member holding a pension were suggested as expendable. All the same, both of these constituents passed muster and were not considered disposable. However, legal aliens, numbering as many as 1,200 in Milwaukee County alone, were among the first to be dropped. A letter from the county board of the CWA informed them that only American citizens or those who had taken out their first papers, indicating an intention to become naturalized, would be employed on federal civil works programs. Workers who appeared to be slothful were also considered for extinction. In many localities throughout the state workers absented themselves from work without notifying the job foreman. It was suggested that a rule be adopted that would trigger automatic dismissal for any workers with two unannounced days of leave. The hope was that by taking these kind of measures it would cushion the reduction quotas established by the CWA.[30]

The editor of the *Oshkosh Northwestern* strode into the topic of quota reductions the following day, January 9, by acknowledging that reductions were not only unavoidable but desirable in some cases. There were those who probably did not need the work, the editor opined, "and they should be weeded out." In other cases, there were those who had "some kind of pull, political or otherwise," and they, too, "should be separated from CWA jobs." However, the reductions translated into a "plunge back into the pool of despair" for thousands of families who had been revitalized by the breadwinners of their families receiving pay for their work. Warming up to the logic of his own reasoning, the editor put in a plug for Winnebago County, and the city of Oshkosh, in particular, arguing that some jurisdictions had a "greater need for CWA employment than others." In certain places, industries had been "hit harder than others by the economic difficulties and are not recovering as fast as others." This allowed the editor to cite Oshkosh as a prime example. The major part of the "heavy costs of unemployment relief have been due to the loss of steady jobs in the woodworking factories," he pointed out, and consequently Oshkosh with its large industrial population "should not be expected to make a larger sacrifice" than other communities where the working population was smaller and the need for jobs less pressing.[31]

The near hysteria created by word that reductions were going into effect was soothed by news that the cuts would not be so drastic and that projects underway would not be tampered with in any material way. In fact, opportunities for those outside of the laboring class were opened up on February 12, 1934. A call went out that day for applicants to the Civil Works Service (CWS). It asked aspiring job-seekers to register, file a personal history, and outline work for which they felt best suited. The CWS projects were designed to absorb professional people, nurses, teachers, clerical workers, and women who were eligible for relief. The projects would be of a "service or social nature," and thus were "not concerned with construction."[32]

Through the winter and spring of 1934, weekly updates on the projects underway, the CWA payrolls, and the impact on relief lists throughout the county were duly reported in the *Oshkosh Northwestern*. Harry Hopkins sent out the word in mid-February that the program was going to start demobilizing in earnest. No new projects would be contemplated, and those in progress would begin a process of tapering off. For the time being, work hours for workers would remain at twenty-four but there was no guarantee how long that would last. It was expected that each week through April would witness a 10% reduction in the work force with a total phasing out by May 1. Those who had other resources would be the first stricken from the payrolls. The report published on February 17 was typical of those throughout this period. The official estimate of federal dollars pumped into Winnebago County was put at $520,495.84. The number of workers employed on CWA projects to date listed Oshkosh in the lead with 1,163 men on payroll. The county itself had 166 men employed, Menasha 193, Neenah 173 and a variety of townships topping off at 331. Omro with 29 employees and Winneconne with 14, both villages, completed the list.[33]

Winnebago County took stock of itself in the spring of 1934 as the CWA funding began to evaporate. Nearly everyone was quite impressed. Neenah completed its projects in due course, including the dredging of the Fox River channel and the clean-up of lower Lake Butte des Morts. In addition to those projects already proposed, Neenah also put men to work grading streets, painting and renovating the interior of the public library and constructing a concrete wall along the water front in the rear of this building. Cold weather made some of the landscaping improvements in the parks a difficult chore and the actual replanting of trees was postponed until the spring. The dirt needed for filling along the river was taken from the side of hills where frost had not yet set. At its height, the CWA employed over 500 Neenah men and every effort was made to employ Neenah residents only. It was reported that a large number of transients sought work during this time but none were hired. The infusion of nearly $6,000 weekly into the economy had salutary effects in the local business sector. Neenah's neighbor, Menasha, experienced similar results in kind, scale and impact.[34]

No other place in the county benefited as much, compliments of the CWA, as did the city of Oshkosh. When the *Oshkosh Northwestern* conducted its evaluation of the CWA experience, it could point to impressive achievements and considerable advantages to the local economy and citizen fortunes. The projects of the CWA "employed a large number of men in the city and a great deal of work was done that might not otherwise have been completed for years." One of the first projects undertaken was the remodeling of Armory B on the corner of Jefferson and Merritt streets. The old stage was removed and the drill floor was expanded. It also received a meticulous cleaning and repainting. Ten men were employed for several weeks cleaning, painting and redecorating city hall and the two public libraries. Another 53 men were employed in the premier project--the renovation of the high school athletic field. There a new drainage system was installed. The field was graded and prepared for seeding that would take place later in the spring. In addition, a cinder running track and straight-away were laid and two tennis courts were roughed out. But the work on Memorial Park employed the most men of any project. Some 200 men braved cold temperatures to work on grading, drainage and sewer systems, and the construction of a bridal path along the river front which was also rip-rapped for erosion control. The workers were also responsible for the building of two hardball and six softball diamonds, a running track, and the preliminary laying out of a football field. Two shuttle board courts, a soccer field, and a swimming pool rounded out this ambitious undertaking.[35]

But it was an added project that ended up employing as many men as the Memorial Park construction. The municipal golf course would eventually employ upwards of 250 men in a labor-intensive effort. A huge amount of landfill was hauled to the course in order to level off many of the low depressions that pockmarked the course and to enable the contouring of bunkers, greens and tees. Cosmetic work on the course would be required later in the spring.

More men were employed on a host of auxiliary projects. Some fifteen were engaged in removing tree stumps from the street terraces throughout the city. Another force of 33 men was given general street improvement projects throughout the months of the CWA. Another 20 were assigned to improving the beaches and docks in Menominee Park. Nearly 55 men were employed in the digging of a drainage ditch along the city's north side (Murdock Street) which would carry run-off water to the lake. More men were engaged to rip out the old streetcar rails on New York Avenue between High Street and Algoma Boulevard. At Riverside Cemetery, a work detail repaired the chapel, enlarged the sexton's office and repainted the facility. The clearing of sewer outlets in West Algoma, lagoon-dredging in South Park, and several smaller projects rounded out the list. Two state-sponsored CWA projects added more men to the payrolls in Oshkosh. Renovation and repainting at the State Teacher's College and preliminary work in construction of an airport were performed just as CWA funding began to run out.[36]

Oshkosh and the rest of Winnebago County derived great satisfaction and secured significant benefits from the CWA program which began on November 15, 1933 and came to an official close on April 1, 1934. The work itself materially improved the quality of life in the county. The salaries generated by CWA payrolls enabled many to channel money back into the economy through purchases that had long been postponed. According to one study conducted by Professor P. G. Fox of the University of Wisconsin, businesses in small cities like Neenah and Menasha, reported sales increases between 25 and 30 percent. City officials who had looked to the winter of 1933-1934 with dread rejoiced in the decrease of those strictly on the dole system of relief. Moreover, taxpayers were given a momentary respite from sharp increases in their tax assessments. The benefits accrued by workers who were gainfully employed and providing for their families for the first time in months are simply incalculable.[37]

Notes

1. *MR*, March 22, 1933.
2. *MR*, March 11, 1933.
3. Michael B. Katz, *In the Shadow of the Poorhouse: A Social History of Welfare in America*, Tenth Anniversary Edition. (NY: Basic Books, 1996), *p. 219*.
4. Katz, *In the Shadow of the Poorhouse*, p. 220.
5. Katz, *In the Shadow of the Poorhouse*, p. 221.
6. Katz, *In the Shadow of the Poorhouse*, p. 225.
7. Katz, *In the Shadow of the Poorhouse*, p. 226.
8. Katz, *In the Shadow of the Poorhouse, pp. 226-28*.
9. Katz, *In the Shadow of the Poorhouse*, pp. 228-29.
10. Martin quoted in Michael O'Brien, *Neenah-Menasha: An Oral History* (Neenah: n.p., 1976), p. 14.
11. *Fox Valley Free Press*, November 18, 1933.
12. SHSW, *Field Report of Florence Peterson, Industrial Commission. August 3, 1932*, in Division of Public Assistance. County Administrative File, 1932-1967, Series 1406, Box No. 130, Folder 70. Roddis is quoted in *Oshkosh Northwestern, November 11, 1932*.
13. SHSW, *L. J. Howman to Florence Peterson, October 10, 1933 and Florence Peterson to L. J. Howman, October 20, 1933* in Wisconsin Department of Public Assistance,

County Administrative File, 1932-1967, Series 1406, Box No. 128, Folder 70-1: Winnebago County Administrative Correspondence.
14. Young quoted in *Oshkosh Northwestern*, November 22, 1933; SHSW, *Letter of C. O. Allen to A. J. Altmeyer, February 4, 1933*, in Wisconsin Division of Public Assistance, County Administrative File, 1932-1967, Series 1406, Box No. 128, Folder 70-0a.
15. SHSW, *Florence Peterson to State Senator Thomas M. Duncan, August 25, 1932* in Wisconsin Division of Public Assistance, County Administrative File, Series 1406, Box No. 130, Folder 70, Correspondence of Oshkosh City Group.
16. SHSW, *Field Report of Florence Peterson, August 3, 1932* in Wisconsin Division of Public Assistance, County Administrative File, 1932-1967, Series 1406, Box No. 130, Folder 70: Menasha.
17. SHSW, *Field Report of Ms. Dresden, June 7, 1933* in Wisconsin Division of Public Assistance, County Admin. File, 1932-1967, Series 1406, Box No. 128, Folder 70-0a.
18. SHSW, *Field Report of Ms. Dresden, June 7, 1932* in Wisconsin Division of Public Assistance, County Admin. File, 1932-19678, Series 1406, Box No. 128, Folder 70-0a.
19. Debate summarized in the *Oshkosh Northwestern*, November 22, 1933.
20. Ryan S. Johnson, Shawn Kantor, and Price V. Fishback, "Striking at the Root of Crime: The Impact of Social Welfare Spending on Crime during the Great Depression," *National Bureau of Economic Research*. Series NBER Working Papers, No. 12825, 2007. In their abstract the authors concluded that "relief spending during the Great Depression lowered property crime in a statistically and economically significant way." For Chief Gabbert's anti-crime measures see Michael Goc, *Oshkosh: 150 Years*, pp. 83-84.
21. John Livingstone, *The Importance of Being from Oshkosh*, p. 112; Clarence Jungwirth, "Oshkosh and the Great Depression of the 1930s," p. ii.
22. *Daily News Times*, November 30, 1930; Michael O'Brien, *Neenah-Menasha: An Oral History*, p. 13. Scanlon would later serve as mayor of Menasha between 1946 and 1956.
23. The project and the fallout are well addressed in Michael Goc, *Oshkosh: 150 Years*, pp. 84-87. Genal's case was heard in Winnebago County Circuit Court. See UWO-ARC, *General Index of Circuit Court, Winnebago County, 1926-1938*. Winnebago Series 118, Vol. 36, Case No. 19135, p. 394.
24. *Oshkosh Northwestern*, May 2, 1931.
25. Michael Goc, *Oshkosh: 150 Years*, p. 171.
26. SHSW, *Wisconsin Division of Public Assistance*, County Administrative File, 1932-1967, Series 1406, Box No. 130, Folder 70; *Oshkosh Northwestern*, December 29, 1933.
27. *Oshkosh Northwestern, October 28 and November 2, 1933*.
28. *Oshkosh Northwestern*, November 12 and November 14, 1933.
29. Figures on the impact the CWA had in Oshkosh were provided by Captain John D. Spencer, the new director of the Federal Relief Center. See *Oshkosh Northwestern*, November 18 and December 30, 1933.
30. See *Letter to N.J. Williams, December 6, 1933* in Wisconsin Department of Public Assistance, County Administrative Files, 1932-1967, Series 1406, Box No. 128, Folder 70-1; *Oshkosh Northwestern*, January 8, 1934. Strikers in Oshkosh found the heavy hand of the law come crashing down on them when they struck at their worksites in November 1933. Oshkosh Police Chief Gabbert had six young men arrested for violating a new vagrancy ordinance. According to John Spencer of the Industrial Commission, he did not "anticipate any trouble" from this action. See *Random Note, dated November 13, 1933* in

Wisconsin Department of Public Assistance, County Administrative Files, 1932-1967, Series 1406, Box No. 128, Folder 70-1.
31. *Oshkosh Northwestern*, January 9, 1934.
32. *Oshkosh Northwestern*, February 13, 1934.
33. *Oshkosh Northwestern*, February 16-17, 1934.
34. *Oshkosh Northwestern*, December 30, 1933 and March 17, 1934.
35. *Oshkosh Northwestern*, March 30, 1934.
36. A complete list of the CWA projects performed in Oshkosh can be found in the *Oshkosh Northwestern*, March 31 and April 5, 1934.
37. *Oshkosh Northwestern*, April 11, 1934.

Chapter 7

1935-1937: Putting People to Work

Winnebago County's anxiety over life in the post-CWA age was apparently well-founded. Many of the positive gains experienced in the first half of 1934 receded as the year moved to its close. Not only had the CWA faded into pleasant memory but FERA, too, went by the boards before the year expired. The second half of 1934 proved to be a period of economic limbo, as one work relief program drew to a close and the next remained in the wings. The prevailing mood was one of pessimism and despair. Nearly five full years of depression had settled on Winnebago County and no apparent end was in sight. Even the ever-hopeful editor of the *Oshkosh Northwestern* strained to apply a happy face on the situation as he put the old year 1934 to rest and mused on the possibilities for 1935:

> This newspaper faces 1935 with a confidence and hope that it will be a year substantially better than 1934. The coming year, we believe, will witness still further advance in rehabilitation. There are many obstacles still in the path and many serious problems yet to be solved. And unemployment continues to be the major hurdle to overcome.[1]

Even before the death of the CWA had been sounded, the various municipalities of Winnebago County wrestled with the renewed problem of dealing with relief. In reply to a letter written by George Oaks, Oshkosh's mayor, Alfred Briggs, State Director of Unemployment Relief, spelled out the new stipulations for managing affairs once the CWA drew to a close. The City of Oshkosh, like any other city in the county and state, "would be expected to carry 50% of the work relief payroll just as it carries 50% of regular relief," Briggs pointed out. All other work relief related costs, such as materials, equipment, teams, trucks, supervision and accident compensation insurance would also be the city's responsibility. Workers under the new program would be permitted up to 24 hours of work per week at the prevailing rate of wages. No worker would be permitted to work more hours than were necessary to enable him to meet his relief needs.

As expected, the only qualified workers on these projects would be those drawn from the regular relief rolls.²

In part, the revised terms for work relief programs were a result of prevailing criticisms of the CWA at the national level. Many of the public improvements performed under the program were categorized as "useless," that is, they were perceived as much ado about nothing. Other critics thought that more men were assigned to projects than were actually warranted, and so the joke went, that men were paid to pass shovels to one another. Franklin Roosevelt had also been stung by criticism from conservative quarters that the administration was promoting a socialist welfare state. And some were alarmed that men who received government wages for minimal labor would be robbed of initiative and morale. The president, then, wanted a plan that would "provide work programs in and near industrial communities" that would "not interfere with private industry and that will be confined to those needy who are unemployed."³

In a hastily called committee of the whole, Oshkosh's aldermen voiced determination to join other cities throughout the state in protesting the new arrangements for relief. They called for a "more equitable" program that would ease the pressure upon the burgeoning tax assessments planned for the next budget year. Members of the council asked the federal government to assume 75% of the relief responsibility so that the monies allocated for relief in 1934 would last until the end of the year. According to C.A. Wiechering, president of the council, local conditions were "worse than at any previous period since the industrial depression." Furthermore, added Mayor Oaks, the city was dealing with the "largest delinquent tax return in the history of the city and unless these taxpayers can be gainfully employed, our task of reemploying all the unemployed is a hopeless one." The committee resolved to wait until action was taken by the Wisconsin League of Municipalities before accepting or rejecting the intended relief program for Oshkosh. They would discover, however, that they had very little choice in the matter.⁴

The de-escalation of public relief work had an almost predictable result. The first week of May 1934 saw some 1,548 families listed on the Oshkosh relief rolls and over a third of them were from the ranks of former taxpayers. The traditional industrial base in Oshkosh was simply not in a position to turn things around unless there was an increased demand in the home building market and that was not to be. In late 1934 the woodworking mills and plants, for all intents and purposes, were shut down. The Badger Lumber Company, purchased in 1924 by the Dearborn Company, had been limping along for some time and the only thing that prevented sealing up the plant was that it had turned its energies to producing specialty products, in this case, the reproduction of colonial era-styled furnishings. Its management gambled that with a limited line of furniture and a small payroll, the company might survive. Though its dinette sets sold for a paltry $6 during the midst of the depression, it at least "weathered the 30s." The Morgan Company hunkered down during the depression years. It ran its plant far below its capacity. While it barely made it through the worst of times, it did so, by keeping its staffing levels at the minimum. The Paine Lumber

Company, formerly the city's largest single employer, enjoyed one last triumph, receiving a contract from the CCC to build some sixty prefabricated shelters, barracks, stores and hospital buildings for workers in the north woods of Minnesota. If the truth be told, the company could have built shelters and the like for every single CCC camp in the nation and still run under capacity. This meager bonus ran its course and the Paine Lumber Company shut down entirely by the close of 1935. It would not resume operations until late 1937.[5]

Even the paternal Menasha Woodenware Company faced hard times by 1935. The company traditionally had manufactured a variety of wooden products, such as butter tubs, packaging materials, boxes and wooden pails. Up to 1920 the market had been kind and the demand for the company's products remained high. But even before the onset of the Great Depression, the industry was moving towards paper-based corrugated boxes and containers. By 1935 the woodenware division within the company was rendered obsolete. Despite being a small operation, the company retained its woodenware personnel and kept operating the factory to preserve jobs. This division was whittled down over the years by mere attrition in the work force; when someone retired or moved on the position was eliminated. It was ultimately dissolved in 1957 when the last of its employees retired.[6]

The dominance of traditional industries within the county translated into an economy that was sluggish, an unemployment problem that was monstrous, and a decline in spending power that was conspicuous. Labor reports for the month of January 1936 were revealing. Factory employment throughout the state was decidedly better than in previous reports. It was 8.2% better than the last month of the previous year and 48.3% better than in the depths of depression in December 1932. Statewide, the per capita weekly earnings of factory workers advanced steadily since the end of 1932, from $15.30 to $20.09. Similar improvements were noted in the increase in the sales forces of retail trades and the value of building contracts awarded in the state. Yet whatever amelioration was being experienced on a statewide basis seemed to elude Winnebago County. The reports for the months of January and February 1936 were instructive. In virtually every category the industries of Neenah-Menasha and Oshkosh trailed off by comparison to the last month of 1934. Comparing January 1936 with December 1934, the percentage of employees on payrolls in Neenah-Menasha dropped 1% and 2.3% in Oshkosh. February witnessed further decreases with Neenah-Menasha reporting a 4.1% drop and Oshkosh coming in at a 2.4% decrease. More telling, however, was the aggregate decline in per capital weekly earnings. In January 1936 factory workers in Neenah-Menasha earned an average of $26.44 per week. In March that figure fell to $23.51. Similarly, the Oshkosh worker could claim an average of $21.36 in January 1936. Two months later, that same worker would garner $18.35 as an average weekly salary. Fluctuations in these reports throughout the years 1935 and 1937 can be accounted for by the vagaries of seasonal demands but the general trend remained unchanged. Factory output and employee hiring and earnings remained stagnant at best and distressed at worst. The area's employment situation would not improve until the following year.[7]

If traditional industries were still at the mercy of a flaccid economy the county was having no better fortune in attracting new businesses. In 1935 the city of Oshkosh scored one victory when the Duo-Safety Ladder Company was lured from Chilton and moved its operation to Oshkosh, taking up residence in the south side near the Morgan Company. Yet stories of business forfeitures always outnumbered the few additions to the business sector. Such was the fate of the Lake States Ink Company founded in Neenah and Menasha in 1933. Raymond A. Kerley, an enterprising printing craftsman, believed that a new form of mega-printing, heat-set letterpress was going to revolutionize the print ink industry. Leaving his job with Cuneo Press in Milwaukee, he opened the new plant in Winnebago County. But Kerley's ambitions could not overcome the ravages of the depression, and like many other small enterprises, the company folded in 1935.[8]

Five years into the Great Depression the cumulative effect of despair and bad fortune was taking its human toll. Although the population of Winnebago County increased by over 2,000 people during the Thirties, the City of Oshkosh registered a slight decline during this period. In the census of 1930 the city was home to some 40,108 souls. The dearth of steady jobs led some to return to family homes outside of the city or it sent others to more promising places. Consequently, the census of 1940 counted 39,089 residents in the city. Oshkosh would not return to the population level of 1930 until 1945.[9] Other indicators of stability, home mortgages and business loans, were also severely shaken by the poor economy in the county. A review of property foreclosure cases and lien foreclosures showed an average of 50 cases heard in the Winnebago County Circuit Court in the four years leading up to the onset of the depression, whereas the average during the depression years through 1938 was a whopping 352 per year. Scores of workers who had been able to manage payments on modest homes before 1930 found themselves unable to do so without paying jobs. Work relief projects only helped some meet their financial obligations.[10]

Perhaps, a more insidious deterioration of society was making the rounds of Winnebago County as it was throughout the entire nation. By 1935 the Great Depression was eroding the very foundations of American culture, creating a profound sense of hopelessness and disruption that ate away at the fabric of family and community. The father's accepted role as provider and head of the household became more problematic and tenuous as idle men spent their days searching for any kind of work. In many cases the familiar rhythms of family life and gender expectations were turned upside down, as the man of the house remained unemployed for long periods and wives and mothers found themselves the breadwinners. Some men suffered anxiety and a feeling or worthlessness for failing to provide for their families. This sense of despair was compounded when families found themselves evicted from homes or compelled to go on the dole. For some the pressure proved too great and they sought the release that suicide afforded. More attention has been paid to those Wall Street brokers who jumped from window sills when the Crash of 1929 wiped out their investments than to the countless numbers who ended their lives of quiet desperation in the midst of the depression. Whereas reports of suicide were frequently blurred or omitted altogether in obituaries, it is clear that no place was spared this consequence of hard times. On November 6, 1933 the *Oshkosh Northwestern* reported that a Neenah resident hanged himself. "Despondency brought on by unemployment," prompted a 56 year-old man to commit suicide in his garage. The human face of the Great Depression is sometimes obscured by the great economic disaster it was.[11]

If the county's principal agenda for the years 1935-1937 was finding a way to put people to work, news of the passage of the Works Progress Administration (WPA) in April 1935 was greeted with considerable enthusiasm. Headed by Harry Hopkins, the WPA provided employment and income to the unemployed during the remainder of the Great Depression. The program built many public buildings, projects and roads, and operated large arts, drama, media and literacy programs. It fed children and distributed food, clothing and housing to the needy. Although scaled back in 1939, and closed for good during the war boom in 1943, the myriad programs of the WPA added up to the largest employment sector in the country--in fact, the largest cluster of government employment opportunities in most states. Eligibility was limited only to one's need for a job. Workers were to be restricted to no more than 30 hours per week but many projects involved months in the field, with workers eating and sleeping on worksites.

In July 1935 an official statement was circulated throughout the nation, espousing specific fundamental principles upon which the WPA would operate. The most salient requirements were that projects should be useful and of a public nature and that a "considerable proportion of the money spent will go into wages for labor." Moreover, the projects needed to be of a character that would "give preference to those on the relief rolls...and to do so in the shortest time possible."[12] Approximately 75% of WPA employment and expenditures went to public facilities and infrastructure, such as highways, streets, public buildings, airports, utilities, small dams, sewers, parks, city halls, public libraries and recreational fields. Nationally, the WPA built over 650,000 miles of road, 78,000 bridges, 125,000 buildings and 700 miles of airport runways. Seven percent of the budget was allocated to arts projects, presenting 225,000 concerts to audiences totaling 150 million, and producing almost 475,000 pieces of art. Ninety percent of the WPA projects were reserved for unskilled blue-collar workers, but it also included many unemployed white-collar workers, artists, musicians, actors, doctors, and writers in such endeavors as the Federal Theatre Project and the Federal Writers Project.[13]

Of all the WPA-sponsored projects in the mid-to-late Thirties, general highway and ancillary infrastructure designs snared the lion's share of funding and hiring in Winnebago County. The start of the Great Depression forced the Highway Department in the county to face drastically reduced budgets. State and Federal aid for highways was cut and Winnebago County was compelled to contemplate pay cuts and reduced hours for its employees. In 1933 the County Board suspended all new highway work and pondered whether this suspension would have to be extended for several years. The budget for fiscal year 1934 brought no amelioration to the dilemma, as another ban on construction was passed again. Worse, yet, the board forbade the purchase of any new equipment for that year. Fortunately, the inauguration of the WPA in 1935 began to reverse this disastrous slide.[14]

The Highway Department became the leading beneficiary of the flow of federal monies. In large part this was because highway and road projects directly addressed the fundamental requirements of the WPA and were, thus, easily justifiable. Virtually no highway or road proposals were denied or later rescinded during the existence of the program. Consequently, public works would do what private industry could not and what was needed most in Winnebago County--it would put people to work. Forty years earlier progressive lobbyists had deemed the payment of road taxes through human labor as "barbarous," reminiscent of the royal corvée of Bourbon France. Federal taxes now employed people to improve the infrastructure of the nation, which, in turn, generated taxable income.

The Project Card File Records for WPA projects, sponsored both by the county-at-large or the individual municipal jurisdictions testify to the myriad work programs approved for funding that started in 1935. That the underlying intention of the projects was to put men into the work force was underscored by the State Highway Commission's insistence that monies would be prioritized for those projects "requiring the maximum of human labor in lieu of machinery whenever practicable." Even a job site where the use of unskilled labor was likely to be minimal, like the building of the Winneconne Bridge, required some provision for "make work," a term coined during the Great Depression.[15] Moreover, despite the availability of mechanical means of grinding limestone into gravel mix, the projects demanded that the traditional method be invoked where workers would manually crush large rocks into smaller ones, and then further reduce them into gravel. In one case in December 1936, approval was given for $7,000 for a county-wide project to "grind limestone and dig marl and sludge for agricultural purposes throughout Winnebago County." The proposal had been earlier rejected because it suggested using mechanical crushers but was approved when the budget was revised to place the emphasis on labor costs. Of the $7,000 granted, a scant $100 was slated for "other costs" than labor. The final product was an inexpensive soil additive or fertilizer furnished to county farmers.[16] This scheme proved to be a repetitive one. On August 4, 1938 the WPA approved a funding request for $76,935 to "quarry and pulverize limestone and dig marl or paper mill sludge, for distribution to farmers," and, again, a mere $550 was reserved for the budgeting of issues other than labor.[17]

In a rather ironic twist, the hardships of the Depression era worked to the advantage of the County Highway Department. Plans that had proven to be pipe dreams in the years prior to the onslaught of hard times now became achievable due to the surge of federal funding. In 1935 the county was awarded $250,000 to begin a long-postponed improvement of railroad crossings. Highway laws of the early 20th century stipulated that the railroads themselves were responsible for the upgrading and maintenance even of crossings. The railroads purposefully dragged their feet in this regard. On one hand, such work would add considerably to their operating expenses and why should they assist competition from trucking companies by furnishing them with better roads? It was not uncommon for the railroads to stall improvements by taking single cases to litigation all the way to the state supreme court. A handful of crossings throughout the county were notoriously perilous but the rail lines rebuffed the County Board's requests to reduce the hazards. Changes in the law and the presence of federal funding ended the impasse once and for all. The County Highway Department and the WPA took over maintenance of the crossings.[18]

Another ambitious county-wide project approved for funding was the repairing, reconstructing and general improvement of Farm to Market roads. This grant resolved a decades-long conflict between individual towns and the county itself. Small towns and villages had routinely petitioned the county to take over the administration of secondary roads but the Board had passed an ordinance halting such transfers. Moreover, the Board had decreed that all these roads be widened a full 20 feet. One grant, amounting to $103,357 in May 1938 called for the reconstruction and relocation of county-owned roads. The tasks, requiring significant labor, would involve "grading, filling, building ditches, draining, constructing and installing culverts and bridges, installing guard rails, and other protective devices." A WPA infusion of 10 million dollars into the state coffers enabled counties like Winnebago to undertake the task of bringing secondary roads up to code.[19]

The county was not the only beneficiary of WPA largesse. Individual municipalities within the county sliced their fair share of the fiscal pie. Neenah, for instance, repeatedly received funds for street, gutter and sidewalk improvements. In February 1937, $11,628 was awarded by the WPA for the improvement of the city's Commercial Street, including the removal of brick pavement, curbs, gutters and the widening and paving of the street. Several months later the city was, again, granted a healthy $12,208 to construct sidewalks on all city-owned property. And in July 1937, Neenah received $18,312 more to construct sidewalks on all city-owned property.[20] While the three largest jurisdictions in the county, the cities of Oshkosh, Neenah and Menasha predictably submitted requests for road construction funding, smaller towns proved no less vigorous. In Omro, a request to "construct sidewalks, curbs and gutters…along with public thoroughfares throughout the village," was approved with a tidy budget of $11,350.[21]

If streets and highways could be built, restored and expanded, they could also easily be beautified. In October 1935 the city of Menasha offered to make "improvements and beautification" of its highways and streets by "trimming and planting along various streets." The nature of the work met with the approval of the WPA. It would require roughly 48% unskilled labor, 12% with intermediate skills, approximately 32% skilled laborers and 7% supervisory staff. The project secured $13,896 and put several dozen men to work for a two month period. And so, truck drivers, common laborers, tree pruners, a tree surgeon and foremen were immediately put to work.[22]

One of the more interesting, and sometimes humorous, aspects to the proposals submitted for approval were the "justification clauses," and some municipalities took creative license in framing them. Menasha's bid for street beautification was predicated on the contention that the "trees have not been trimmed for some time and are becoming hazardous to pedestrians." One might wonder why this work was not done earlier, and why individual citizens or city workers could not be assigned a task like this one. Apparently, the need to place people in paying jobs was paramount and overrode all other considerations. Other justifications cited logic that was either specious in character or made claims that lacked any credible evidence or statistical data. In a preliminary request that would eventually lead to the complete reconstruction of its principal municipal park, Menasha requested and received $18,200 on January 10, 1936 for an expansion to its Park and Recreation facilities. Without any evidence or hard data detailing the nature of the problem nor how the proposal would ameliorate it, Menasha averred that the "lack of park and recreation space is leading to child delinquency...we are in need of 50 additional acres to fulfill this purpose."[23]

Despite the impressive funding that road construction projects attracted, there were numerous other ways to secure funds and put people to work. Sewage, sanitation and general environmental improvements, tasks that were both clearly not the routine responsibility of municipal workers and which bore a cost that made most other cities shudder even in more prosperous times, were now fair game during the WPA years. General sanitation issues had for some time been in the forefront of county discussion even before the Great Depression but very little had been done to address the outstanding issues. Moreover, sewer systems varied greatly within the county at large. Larger municipalities like Menasha, Neenah and Oshkosh had both storm and sewage systems but expanded use of the latter had outstripped the ability to properly dispose of waste. People in small townships generally had septic systems, some of which had environmentally sensitive drainage fields, others tended to flow precariously close to sources of potable water. In the more rural regions of the county, the antiquated outhouse system proved to be the old and reliable way of dealing with human discharge.

That municipal sewer systems were becoming taxed beyond their capacities came home to Oshkosh several times in the decade of the Twenties. In 1924, during a torrential downpour, the disposal plant at Campbell Creek proved unable to handle the volume of storm runoff and sewage funneling into its works. Consequently, the fouled water had no recourse but to begin backing up into the streets of the city. Citizens of the time could remember that intersections were flooded to waist-high levels and the pungent smell of offal was dreadful. And the streets were not the only repository of sewage runoff. Flooded streets close to the Fox River and Lake Winnebago freely drained into these waters, elevating the quality of water to the toxic level.

In 1933 a scientist, Dr. Carl A. Harper, spoke to the Oshkosh city council and condemned the "bad condition" of the water in the lake. "I have heard some complaints from up here about the amount of chlorine in the water and the bad taste it leaves," he intoned, "well, unless you get a new system of sewerage disposal that bad taste is going to keep right on getting worse." Harper suggested that Oshkosh's system needed a series of intercepting sewers that would conduct water directly to a treatment plant or disposal point. In fact there had been an interceptor built along Hazel Street, and while it did divert sewage run off from going into the lake, it unfortunately channeled it into the Fox River at Moore Street. The wishful thinking of the time was that the waste would become diluted and harmless once it made its way into the lake, as if out of sight--out of mind. Compounding this scenario was the fact that there was absolutely no protection against sewer runoff south of the Fox as it emptied into the lake. Dr. Harper disapproved of these arrangements and disparaged the beaches at Menominee Park, warning that those who did not immediately rinse off after bathing in the lake were risking their health because of high bacterial content in the water. Despite the apocalyptic-like warnings of Dr. Harper, the city council saw no way to raise the monies necessary for so monumental a project. All of this would change in 1935 when the Federal government stepped in.[24]

The agreement reached between the City of Oshkosh and the WPA was that federal monies would cover 45% of the budget costs for a major overhaul of the city's sanitation facilities. To cover the balance, the city issued bonds, payable in 1965, to cover its share of a staggering $900,000 bill. Engineers went about designing a sanitary system that would serve a population of 70,000 people. Multiple interceptor lines would be laid to divert all sewage towards the plant. And the waste treatment plant at Campbell Creek would be completely redesigned and rebuilt. The individual tasks comprising the sum total of the project were proposed and approved in incremental steps according to standard WPA protocol. Thus, periodic proposals, like the one approved on August 21, 1936, "to lay sanitary and storm sewers on various streets in the City of Oshkosh...exclusive of projects specifically approved," with a hefty budget of $33,846, were more or less repeated time and again. The result is that by the time the Thirties ended, the city of Oshkosh had a state of the art sanitary system and a host of workers enjoyed employment during the difficult times.[25]

The county's other two cities, Neenah and Menasha, received slightly smaller awards for sanitary modernization. Menasha, for example, received a large grant, totaling $92,463 to construct storm and sanitary sewers and water drains, including manholes, catch basins, hydrants and pumping stations throughout the streets of the city. Interestingly, one of the peripheral benefits of sanitary projects was that items like manhole covers and other municipal castings helped keep Neenah's foundry in operation. Smaller townships and villages like Omro, Winneconne, and the Town of Oshkosh were not left out of the picture. With less pressing needs for sanitation improvement, these jurisdictions tended to wait until 1938 before funds trickled their way. For example, Winneconne applauded itself and Village Board president, J.W. Meigher, for obtaining "federal grants which pay two-thirds of the cost of the sewer system." An additional grant was awarded in 1939 to complete the construction of a sanitation plant and sanitary sewer system, "with pump houses, clarifiers, valves, sludge beds, siphons, manholes and appurtenances..."[26]

Lest it be thought that conservation and environmental protection might be the "buzz words" of a more contemporary period, the Depression era gave considerable thought to these matters. But until the appearance of the WPA, thought was the only affordable part of making it a reality. Although individual jurisdictions obtained a piece of conservation action, most projects were sanctioned on either a state or county-wide basis. In 1937, a sizeable half-million dollars was allocated to the state "to provide for emergency work when danger to life or grave risk to property is engendered by flood or thaw conditions." And when a similar grant, totaling $300,000 was approved to combat threats posed by wildfires.[27] The county's own bounty was generous as well. In 1936, it was given $80,000 to construct small water conservation dams. In addition to projects that had already been specifically approved, this one would operate on any federal, state, county or municipal property, and even private property, if the work would prove beneficial to the public at large. The following year a grant was garnered that initiated stream and lake improvements. Under this initiative, the county would expand and repair warden quarters facilities, construct and repair boats and boat trailers, build a barge, as well as fish and crib buildings, and also construct shelters, feeding hoppers and stations and facilities for game birds and animals." That same year the county received aid in doing whatever was necessary to remove unwanted rough fish from Lake Winnebago. One wonders whether the irony was lost upon those who had been handed out rough fish to eat just a few years before. One final grant was awarded in 1939 for conservation and environmental protection in the county. Over $80,000 was to be used to conduct general wildlife construction. The work would expand upon efforts begun in 1936 but would also include the building of spawning pens, the making of snow shoes, removal of brush tangles, and the rewiring of one building and the construction of a new administration office. On average, all conservation grants set aside nearly 90% in budgetary labor costs.[28]

The City of Oshkosh apparently believed that conservation and environmental action were not the sole province of the county. In a series of approved projects, the city captured over $65,000 from the state's beneficence. Flooding along Campbell Creek had always been a nagging problem for the city and now the funds were available to institute flood control measures. It hired men to excavate and backfill along the banks of the creek and then construct and install retaining walls. In another, less ambitious undertaking, the city removed debris from along the shores and inlets of Lake Winnebago; flotsam was perceived as a navigational hazard. Another project merely replaced and enlarged funds already approved for major upgrading of the buildings and equipment allocated for use by the state game wardens.[29]

One other land improvement scheme was endorsed by the WPA in 1935 and the city of Oshkosh capitalized on it. Oshkosh had purchased land on the south end of Lake Butte Des Morts at its junction with the Fox River. Cashing in on the growing popularity of the game of golf, a handful of citizens, headed by W. G. Maxcy, began soliciting donations to expand the golf course on that property. By 1921, the first nine holes had already been constructed, but the back nine remained a forlorn hope when the Depression hit. While providing a facility for golfing might have appeared trivial given the hard times, the course was a municipal one and the reasoning for expanding the course contained the key public welfare justifications. By 1936 the course featured eighteen holes. The first club house on the course had been something akin to a military barrack. However, in 1937 the WPA sanctioned and provided over $2000 to frame a new house on the site.[30]

"Repair and Improve" became a catch phrase for work proposals funded by the WPA during the Thirties. Libraries, schools, museums, courts, as well as any institution or facility that served the public were entitled to seek funds to build, expand, repair or simply spruce up the environs. Menasha became one of the earliest beneficiaries of WPA funding. On the evening of March 20, 1936, the city's high school was gutted by fire. A total loss, the school was beyond any hope of salvaging. Students had to be channeled toward other schools in the city. Plans were immediately made to move forward. On April 6, the city was awarded nearly $9,000 to demolish the charred remains of the old school. This involved pulling down walls, leveling floors, removing steel beams and generally razing the building to the ground. In its initial proposal, the city argued that the "appearance of the building...was detrimental to this otherwise beautiful city," and that the blight "should be removed." Later, in August, the city received the go-ahead from the state director of the WPA to request funds for the building of a brand new school. Simultaneously, the city council of Menasha made plans to issue bonds to raise its share of the total cost. The new school was completed by the end of 1937.[31]

While no other jurisdiction experienced the trauma of having one of its school buildings destroyed, most of them were determined to take advantage of the available funding to make long-postponed repairs and improvements. Menasha did not entirely neglect the remaining schools within its district, when in December 1936 the city obtained monies to point the cornice and coping of Butte des Morts school with plastic cement. All schools in the Third Ward would get their roofs covered with an "asbestoline roof coating." Later the city anteed up $7,920 in order to obtain another $23,820 for painting and repairing various schools throughout Menasha. Omro acquitted itself quite well when it was granted $6,856 for general improvement of the school buildings in the village, including the remodeling of the Band and Manual Arts buildings, installing plumbing fixtures in the gymnasium, and constructing school tennis courts. The Town of Oshkosh received funding to improve its school buildings and playgrounds. The work included carpentry, electrical upgrading, masonry and roofing work. Plastering, painting and landscaping added an aesthetic touch.[32]

As in most other arenas of work proposals, the city of Oshkosh refused to lag behind its fellow Winnebago County jurisdictions. An October 1936 request for monies was approved so that the city could expand both the high school's boiler room and a lumber storage room at the Beach School. Consecutive grants were awarded later in 1936 to refinish all of the desks and floors within the school district. The paint brush seems never to have gone dry in Oshkosh. Repeatedly, the city received monies for painting projects. Starting in 1936, and as late as 1940, Oshkosh was handed funding to "improve school buildings and grounds" with projects in "plastering, painting, carpentry masonry, plumbing and electrical work," as well as "improving and installing heating facilities, removing and erecting fences, constructing curbs, tennis courts, walks, driveways and bleachers, and the grading and landscaping" of school grounds.[33] Nor was the State Teacher's College in Oshkosh going to be left out in the cold. Proposed in 1938, and granted in February 1939, the college was bestowed its third generous award in order to perform an array of tasks. A new roof was put on one of its academic buildings. Shower stalls were installed in several buildings. Its science lab was graced by new laboratory tables. One lecture hall was bathed in acoustic tile while general electrical, plumbing and heating improvements were made throughout the college's buildings.[34]

The same "repair and improve" attitude affixed to public schools extended to general infrastructure needs, from federal facilities like post offices, to county services like the sanitarium and court house, to municipal structures like libraries and city garages. Courtesy of a federal grant Oshkosh undertook a general cleaning and painting of the Main Library and the South Side Branch in 1936. That same year monies were obtained to give the city hall a structural overhaul. One of the towers of the hall had rotted to the point of obsolescence and had to be torn down. Workers on this project also repaired the building's parapet, coping, slate roof and warped windows. The following year, 1937, and another WPA award later, funds were provided to completely repaint the edifice. Before the end of the decade, all three cities, Oshkosh, Neenah and Menasha had received assistance in the building of new municipal garages to house their police cars and city trucks.

The city museum in Oshkosh, which at one point early on in the depression cycle thought it might have to close its doors, received a grant, albeit a rather small one, to "paint doors, windows and walls, and to revamp the electrical wiring" in the old mansion, as well as perform cosmetic improvements on the exterior. And Oshkosh received an impressive $83,551 to construct a new fire station and street department garage, while obtaining permission from the federal government to demolish the old Post Office building with the understanding that a replacement would be in the offing. Even municipal cemeteries were swept up in the general improvement schemes. Riverside Park in Oshkosh benefited from a tidy grant to undertake repairs and modernization. In Menasha, a sizeable amount of money was set aside to "construct a chapel, mausoleum, receiving vault, toilets and a storage building" in its city's cemetery.[35]

Most of the proposed projects during the WPA era were clearly delineated along jurisdictional lines. A city garage constructed in Neenah, after all, fell within that city's purview. This was not the case with the Sunnyview Sanitarium, officially located four miles north of the City of Oshkosh. Technically, the facility was located within the Town of Oshkosh's boundaries. Yet, the institution was chartered to serve all the jurisdictions within both Winnebago and Fond du Lac counties. Hence, when proposals were submitted, they were done by the Town of Oshkosh, a town that was in desperate need for employment schemes, but reflected the cumulative weight of consideration from all the jurisdictions involved.

By nearly all accounts, the facilities on the Sanitarium grounds were in dismal condition. Even in better times, it was likely that a mental health facility would receive the short end of the budgetary stick. And, at first, it appeared it was going to experience the same neglect when the federal government began releasing monies under the WPA. While Sunnyview received its first award in July 1936, it was for a paltry amount and was allocated for cosmetic landscaping and curbing concerns on the grounds themselves. Consecutive awards began trickling in throughout 1937 and reached their apex between 1938-1939, possibly because many of the other infrastructure needs of the county had already been addressed. Nonetheless, by the close of 1939, an abundance of federal subsidies had completely transformed the facility. All of the buildings on site received a complete modernization of their infrastructure, including new wiring, plumbing and a new power plant. The new wiring and plumbing necessitated complete reconstruction of building walls, and paint was liberally applied throughout. The grounds were given meticulous attention, including the installation of an underground water sprinkler. By the close of the decade Sunnyview was no longer a source of shame but a symbol of progress and pride.[36]

If the WPA was designed to put people to work and restore a sense of self-esteem and hopefulness, it also tried to address the aesthetic quality of life in order to further buoy human spirits during the Great Depression. In fact, this was already understood as a useful idea, as many of the predecessors of the WPA, the PWA and CWA, had targeted the same goal. One of the easiest and most productive ways to do this was to improve the various parks and public grounds within the county. Much like highway construction, the number of projects aimed at upgrading existing parks and building new ones is simply too large to recapitulate. Omro, for example, made substantial improvements to its village parks, particularly the one downtown by the frontage of the Fox River, where it constructed a boat house, retaining walls and bridges across its distinctive lagoon. Neenah continued many of the landscaping and park maintenance projects of the earliest days of the Depression. Menasha, a genuine working-class town, assiduously directed monies into general park improvements, and with the completion of its new high school, channeled funds into the building of an athletic field on the site. Oshkosh remained determined to make Menominee Park a showcase for the county and in 1938 initiated a general beautification throughout the city, hiring "needy persons" to plant flowers and small shrubs on public property and buildings. Through the auspices of the Town of Oshkosh, the county took the opportunity to renovate the county fairgrounds, then located on Murdock Avenue, between Jackson and Main streets. Sewers and water mains were introduced onto the grounds and new exhibit buildings were constructed. An old and dilapidated barn on the property was razed, and the property was girded by a newly installed fence. The county's numerous and spacious parks of today are a legacy of the Depression era WPA.[37]

If food for the bodies of unemployed was one of the central aims of the many work projects of the era in Winnebago County, nourishment of the soul was not entirely neglected. Even before the onset of the WPA, the federal government had attempted to provide employment for artists on relief. The Public Works of Art Project (PWAP) had operated from 1933 to 1934, and the Treasury Department Section of Painting and Sculpture was created after the demise of PWAP. The drawbacks of these programs was their limited scope and brief existence. The Federal Art Project (FAP) was the art wing of the WPA. Again, the accent would be placed upon art work for viewing by the general public, an enormously democratic and egalitarian stance. It would employ out-of-work artists and provide pieces of public art for non-federal government buildings, county courthouses, post offices, libraries and the like. Over time it would have an extraordinary reach, creating over 5,000 jobs for artists and producing over 225,000 works of art for the American people. Artists labored at their craft for little money but with enormous pride. Their works stand as reminders of a time in the nation's history when dreams and hopes were not allowed to be destroyed by economic disaster.

As the luck of the draw would have it, Winnebago County was not the beneficiary of a great deal of this art work. Some of the most celebrated art of the time were the various murals painted in newly constructed post offices. Although not technically part of the FAP program, it was, nonetheless, representative of the goals of subsidized art during the era. A number of post offices in surrounding areas, like Berlin in Green Lake County and Chilton in Calumet County, were selected for murals. These works, like others during the period, were designed to capture the essence of family and community life. Hence, Berlin's mural, titled, "Gathering Cranberries," celebrated that town's early roots in the cranberry industry. In Oshkosh, the public museum was given a number of art pieces and Swart Hall on the campus of the State Teacher's College was adorned by a large mural in its foyer, featuring a traditional Wisconsin family, albeit a strikingly Nordic-looking one, going about its daily life.[38]

Both the economic health and the prospective hopes of the residents of Winnebago County were tempered by an entrenched ambivalence during the years 1935 and 1936. Clearly, most indicators of economic vitality were better than during the nadir of the previous years but no one was certain that prosperity was just around the corner. The most desperate in the county had their spirits charged by the work projects springing up during these two years, but both they, and those meaningfully employed, seemed to understand that this did not translate into recovery. Meanwhile, taxpayers were chagrined over the increases to their tax assessments which permitted the floating of this artificial economy.

The *Oshkosh Northwestern*, the self-proclaimed barometer of county attitudes and fortunes, projected measured optimism in its end-of-the-year forecasts for the successive years of 1936 and 1937. In qualified tones, smacking more of damning by faint praise, the paper proclaimed that the passing of the year 1935 was "better, on the whole, than that of the preceding one and better in many ways than any of the years in which the economic depression prevailed." "Some progress has been made in the hard, upward climb out of our material troubles," the editor opined, and that the "momentum gained in 1935 and anticipated in 1936 will take us back to recovery and prosperity." Yet, the overall reliance upon pious platitudes, even mushy sentimentalism in the remainder of the editorial betrayed the fact that whatever the indicators of impending economic improvement were, they were not particularly convincing.[39]

A year later, the paper repeated its meek predictions of great economic strides for the new year 1937. This time, however, there was a bit more substance to the prognostication, as relief rolls began to shrink, a marked increase was seen in new hiring at formerly stagnant industries, and the stock market was beginning to rally. Contemplating the "local opportunities and possibilities for the year 1937, the *Oshkosh Northwestern* suggested that some communities were already on their way to recovery. Oshkosh, because of its concentration in the woodworking industry lagged a little behind. Nevertheless, an increase in employment, consumer spending, local banking and post office receipts, railroad car loadings and other activities convinced the paper that substantial gains had been made during 1936 and that there was every reason to believe that the long-anticipated recovery was at hand.[40]

Interestingly, a caveat offered by the editor on this final day of 1936 revealed a better honed forecast of the future than any of the economic projections the paper had made since the onset of the Great Depression. The prosperity and recovery that the editor thought was assured for 1937 would be predicated upon a harmonious relationship between workers and employers. "[The] avoidance of labor disputes is necessary," the paper warned, "for an outbreak of labor difficulties would be a serious blow to progress." The next two years would be marked by significant conflict and dispute between capital and labor and an unforeseen setback in the economy would hurl the nation and Winnebago County along with it back into the depths of depression.[41]

Notes

1. *Oshkosh Northwestern*, December 29, 1934.
2. SHSW, *Alfred W. Briggs to George F. Oaks, March 22, 1934* in Wisconsin Division of Public Assistance, County Administrative Files, 1932-1967, Series 1406, Box No. 128, Folder 70-0a, Winnebago County Field Reports.
3. Reported in the *Oshkosh Northwestern*, March 2, 1934.
4. Meeting reported in the *Oshkosh Northwestern*, March 27, 1934.
5. Steve R. Lankau, *A Thumbnail History of Former City of Oshkosh Firms*, pp. 3, 64. Goc, *Oshkosh: 150 Years*, p. 84.

6. Richard Blodgett, *Menasha Corporation: An Odyssey of Five Generations.* (Lyme, CT: C.T. Greenwood Publishing Group, Inc., 1999), p. 51.
7. *WLMR,* Vol. 16, Nos. 1-3, January-March 1936.
8. "Inside Kerley Ink--People and Production," from an article appearing in the Oct. 1982 issue of *The American Inkmaker,* http://www.kerleyink.com/kerley_story/inside_kerley.html, p. 2.
9. *City of Oshkosh Directory, 1932, p. 14, and* City of Oshkosh Directory, *1942,* p. 24.
10. UWO-ARC, *General Index: Circuit Court of Winnebago County, 1926-1938,* Winnebago Series, Volume 118. Note: This review does not include similar cases heard in the Winnebago County Court. Considerably fewer foreclosure cases were heard in this court, perhaps 10-15% of those heard in the circuit court. But a cursory review of those records appears to bear similar results. See *General Index: Winnebago County Court, 1926-1938.* Winnebago Series 127, vol. 2.
11. *Oshkosh Northwestern,* November 6, 1933. While not tabulated, a review of divorce cases heard in the Winnebago County Circuit Court during the years of the Great Depression indicates that a considerable increase over the final years of the prior decade. However, it would be speculative to suggest any direct cause and effect in this matter. See *General Index: Circuit Court of Winnebago County,1926-1938,* Winnebago Series, Vol. 18. Also, in a telephone interview, a man in his late teens during the early years of the Great Depression from a very large family related that when he saw that his mother was not eating properly with so many mouths to feed, decided to leave home and seek his fortune on the rails. *Telephone interview with Name-Withheld Resident,* August 19, 2007.
12. SHSW, *Preliminary Statement of Information for Sponsors of Works Progress Administration Projects,* WPA File, State of Wisconsin, Miscellaneous Record, Series 911, Box No. 17, Folder: WPA Safety Bulletins, p. 2.
13. A very concise and useful summary of the WPA can be found in Wikipedia, http://en.wikipedia.org/wike/Works_Progress_Administration.
14. Michael J. Goc, *A History of the Winnebago County Highway Department and Its Roads* (self-published, 1983), p. 21.
15. Goc, *A History of the Winnebago County Highway Department,* p. 22.
16. SHSW, *Federal Records, Works Project Administration, Wisconsin Division,* WPA Project Card File Records, 1936-1942, Series 1688, Box No. 5, Folder: County Wide, See Series Project No. 2D-1179, approved December 15, 1936.
17. SHSW, *Federal Records, Works Project Administration, Wisconsin Division,* WPA Project Card File Records, 1936-1942, Series 1688, Box No. 5, Folder: County Wide, See Series Project No. 2S2033/30259.
18. Michael Goc, *A History of the Winnebago County Highway Department,* pp. 22-23.
19. SHSW, *Federal Records, Work Project Administration, Wisconsin Division,* WPA Project Card File Records,1936-1942, Series 1688, Box No.5, Folder: Statewide Projects. See O.P. 65-53-400-470-280. It should be noted that the frenzy of activity during this period produced ripple effects in the economy. In a history of the City of Oshkosh, one observer notes that the years of the WPA were the busiest in the history of the city's Engineering Department. This department had its office "filled to overflowing with drafting plans, writing specifications, recording the finished work and making applications for additional jobs from the Federal government." See M. Goc, *Oshkosh: 150 Years,* p. 73.
20. SHSW, *Federal Records, Work Project Administration, Wisconsin Division,* WPA Project Card File Records, 1936-1942, Series 1688, Box No. 5, Folder: Neenah. See Project Series Nos. 2D-1393, 2D-1558, and 2D-1648.
21. SHSW, *Federal Records, Work Project Administration, Wisconsin Division,* WPA

Project Card File Records, 1936-1942, Series 1688, Box No. 5, Folder: Town of Omro. See Project Series No. 2D-1888. Menasha's aggressive pursuit of funding to construct "concrete curbs and gutters on various streets" in the city was handsomely rewarded with a working budget of $72,462 in 1936. See SHSW, *Federal Records, Work Project Administration, Wisconsin Division,* WPA Project Card File Records, 1936-1942, Series 1688, Box No. 5, Folder: City of Menasha. See Project Series No. 2D-1181.

22. UWO-ARC, City of Menasha, City Clerk, *City Clerk's Papers, 1855-1964.* WPA File, Winnebago Series 84, Box No. 4, Folder 14.

23. UWO-ARC, City of Menasha, City Clerk, *City Clerk Papers, 1855-1964,* WPA Files, Winnebago Series 84, Box No. 4, Folder 14. It should be noted, however, that the City of Oshkosh failed in its bid to get some tree trimming done with Federal monies. On August 21, 1937, its hopes to trim some 5,000 trees, to plant 1,000 more and to transplant some 100 others was denied. The reason for disapproval: "Trimming trees on city-owned property is considered current maintenance, provision for which should be made in the regular budget of the sponsor." Perhaps, if Oshkosh had submitted this bid a year earlier, as did Menasha, the response might have been in the affirmative. See SHSW, *Federal Records Administration, Work Project Administration, Wisconsin Division,* WPA Project Card File Records, 1936-1942, Series 1688, Box No. 5, File: Miscellaneous.

24. Dr. Harper's presentation can be found in the *Oshkosh Northwestern,* July 13, 1933.

25. SHSW, *Federal Records, Work Projects Administration, Wisconsin Division,* WPA Project Card File Records, 1936-1942, Series 1688, Box No. %, Folder: Streets, Project Series No. 2D-1159.

26. See *Winneconne News,* March 17, 1938. For the 1939 grant, see SHSW, *Federal Records, Works Project Administration, Wisconsin Division,* WPA Project Card File Records, 1936-1942, Series 1688, Box No. 5, Folder: Winneconne, Project Series No. S616, S297.

27. SHSW, *Federal Records, Works Project Administration, Wisconsin Division,* WPA Project Card File Records, 1936-1942, Series 1688, Box No. 5, Folder: Statewide Projects, Project Series Nos. S616, S297.

28. SHSW, *Federal Records, Works Project Administration, Wisconsin Division,* WPA Project Card Files, 1936-1942, Series 1688, Box No. 5, Folder: Winnebago County, Project Series Nos. 2D1404, 2D-1808, 2D-2077, 2D-2244.

29. SHSW, *Federal Records, Works Project Administration, Wisconsin Division,* WPA Project Card Files, 1936-1942, Series 1688, Box No.5, Folder: City of Oshkosh, Project Series Nos. 2D-4429, 2D-1478, 2D-1166.

30. Michael Goc, *One Hundred Years a City,* p. 110. For WPA grant for the club house, see SHSW, *Federal Records, Works Project Administration, Wisconsin Division,* WPA Project Card Files., 1936-1942, Series 1688, Box No. 5, Folder: City of Oshkosh, Project Series No. 2D-1310.

31. *Oshkosh Northwestern,* March 21, 1936. Recovery efforts can be found in UWO-ARC, Menasha City Clerk Office, *City Clerk Papers, 1855-1964,* WPA Files, Winnebago Series 84, Box No. 4, Folder 14.

32. SHSW, *Federal Records, Works Project Administration, Wisconsin Division,* WPA Project Card File Records, 1936-1942, Series 1688, Box No. 5, Folder: Menasha, Project Series Nos. 2D-1611. 2D-1319. Omro's project can be found in the above, Series 1688, Box No. 5, Folder: Omro, Project Series No. 2D-2217, while the Town of Oshkosh work can be found in Series 1688, Box No. 5, Folder: Town of Oshkosh, Project Series No. 2D-2327.

33. SHSW, *Federal Records, Works Project Administration, Wisconsin Division,* WPA Project Card File Records, 1936-1942, Series 1688, Box No. 5, Folder: City of Oshkosh, Project Series Nos. 2D-1334, 2D-1403, 2D-1447.
34. SHSW, *Federal Records, Works Project Administration, Wisconsin Division,* WPA Project File Card Records, 1936-1942, Series 1688, Box No. 5, Folder: City of Oshkosh, Project Series No. 2D-2236.
35. SHSW, *Federal Works Project Administration, Wisconsin Division,* WPA File Card Records, 1936-1942, Series 1688, Box No. 5, Folders: City of Oshkosh and Menasha, Project Series Nos. 2D-1230, 2D-1269, 2D-1666, 2D-1575, 2D-2207, 2D-2263, 2D-1117.
36. SHSW, *Federal Records, Works Project Administration, Wisconsin Division,* WPA Project Card File Records, 1936-1942, Series 1688, Box No. 5, Folder: Town of Oshkosh, Project Series Nos. 2D-1090, 2D-1930, 2D-1521. Four separate projects were proposed (and approved) by Winnebago County and the monies were apportioned to the Winnebago County State Hospital, a facility across the road from the Sanitarium. The work done there largely mirrored the improvements performed at Sunnyview. See reference above, Project Nos. 2D-2073, 2D-1654, 2D1333, 2D-2337.
37. SHSW, *Federal Records, Works Project Administration, Wisconsin Division,* WPA File Card Records, 1936-1942, Series 1688, Box No. 5, Folders: Omro, Neenah, Menasha, Oshkosh, and Winnebago County, Project Series Nos. 2D-1668, 2D-1693, 2D-1910, 2D-1435, 2d-70-2361, 2D-2383, 2D-1885.
38. Post Office murals were subsidized by the Federal Section of Fine Arts, frequently referred to as "the Section."
39. *Oshkosh Northwestern,* December 31, 1935.
40. *Oshkosh Northwestern,* December 31, 1936.
41. *Oshkosh Northwestern,* December 31, 1936.

Chapter 8

1937-1939: The Woes of Labor

The *Oshkosh Northwestern's* closing editorial for the year 1936 was, perhaps, the only one of the previous six years during the Great Depression resembling anything close to the truth. As the new year 1937 opened there were encouraging economic signs both in the national and state arenas, as well as in local Winnebago County. Hopeful news of the national recovery were in abundant circulation in the early months of 1937. While the economy had not rebounded to its 1929 capacity, it was considerably more vibrant than at the lowest point of the Depression between 1932 and 1934. Gross National Production had increased 69% between 1933 and 1937. Average annual earnings had improved from an all-time low of $1,048 in 1933 to $1,258 in 1937. Unemployment was on the wane as well. At its height in 1933 nearly 25% of American workers were out of work, whereas by 1937, this figure had been shaved to 14%. Workers, many of whom were flushed with money from WPA employment, were spending more on consumer goods. Finally, although it was the most suspect of economic indicators, the stock market began a steady incline in the spring of 1936, reaching its apex in April 1937. Only agricultural interests seemed left out of the rosy picture.[1]

To a large extent, Winnebago County was included in this apparent rebound. The twin cities of Neenah and Menasha were reporting diminished relief cases by 1937 and were only concerned that outsiders were flocking to their region in search of employment. With the cry of "strangers on the relief load" reverberating throughout the council chambers of Neenah and Menasha in 1937, relief director Remmel reported that outsiders had been attracted to the twin cities because of an Industrial Commission report that identified Neenah and Menasha as ranking near the top among Wisconsin cities in terms of wages and employment at this stage of the depression. Migrants merely need to establish residency for a period of one year in order to be considered wards of the cities' relief load. Each new arrival, then, could not be returned to the relief office of his former residence and by default became Neenah's and Menasha's responsibility. Remmel described this phenomenon as a menace, particularly since a number of WPA projects were slated for cessation and the added burden of this unemployed migration might have an adverse impact upon the region's relief rolls. Neenah's city council declared that this influx of migrants needed to be stopped as soon as possible. Nonetheless, these two paper mill cities, as one student of the Great Depression there has concluded, weathered these challenges and were nearly impervious to the devastating effects of unemployment and relief needs that plagued so many other places.[2]

One such "other place" was Oshkosh. The general collapse of the woodworking mills had afflicted the city with high unemployment and consistently nagging relief challenges. Here too, however, recovery hopes were sustained by favorable reports. Even though the accurate reporting of the local economy lagged far behind national trends, Department of Commerce reports for the year 1935 were promising. Although not released until April 1937, the report was taken as "further proof that manufacturing in Oshkosh has been making steady progress out of the recent depression." The tale of the tape was repetitious for every indicator. The manufacturing climate was not as comforting as the predepression figures but infinitely better when the bottom dropped out in 1933. The value of industrial production in Oshkosh was reported still to be 42.2% of that in 1929 but 48.4% improved over that disastrous period in 1933. The number of wage earners employed in Oshkosh demonstrated a similar trend. It was still a staggering 41.1% below the 1929 figures but registered a 16.1% increase over 1933 levels.[3]

The statistics regarding the number of manufacturing concerns, the relative value of their production, the wages they paid employees, and the gross profits of employers in Oshkosh revealed additional evidence of an economic upturn. In 1929 Oshkosh tallied 119 industrial concerns and employed a total of 6,572 workers. By 1933 the city reported only 92 firms and employed only 3,337 workers. In 1935, there were 91 industries employing 3,874 persons. The modest employment gain in 1935 over the 1933 figure was testimony to the intractable sluggishness of the home building market, yet, nonetheless, was viewed as an encouraging trend. Oshkosh industries in 1935 were producing more, employing more, paying its employees more and enjoying greater profits than they did in 1933.[4]

Perhaps the most symbolic manufacturing triumph of 1937 was the return of the Paine Lumber Company to the ranks of producers. As the industry's largest employer in 1929 it had been the kingpin of the woodworking world. Its total and utter collapse in 1934 had sent desperate reverberations throughout the city of Oshkosh. Other mills in the city had managed to remain technically open for business. A combination of specialized products and employee downsizing had kept plants like the Morgan Company from closing their doors entirely. Paine seized upon an innovation in 1937 to resuscitate its operations. In preparation for reopening the plant, the company was compelled to sell some of its property to the city of Oshkosh in March. Part of the property sold would eventually be corralled by the intersections of Algoma Boulevard and Congress Avenue, the present day site of Arboretum Park and adorned by a memorial statue of a Spanish-American War volunteer astride a huge boulder. On August 26 the plant

The Woes of Labor

announced it was prepared to launch production of a new door, a lighter and more attractive one. Merchandized under the trade name, "Rezo," it held a French patent. It was a hollow, flush door, having the appearance of a solid wood door, but lighter in weight and construction. It had originally been used on French ocean liners and boasted the additional attraction that it would not warp. By September the first 25 workers were installing the specialized machinery and 100 workers were expected to be on board by November when the plant began operations. Additional employees would be hired once demand for production warranted it.[5]

Yet, for all the positive news afoot in early 1937, public relief statistics belied the rosy picture. Figures for early 1937 appeared to usher in additional tidings of good news, although they were hardly indicators of substantial recovery. The number of those receiving public assistance declined in the second-half of 1936 and this trend continued for the first three months of the following year. Reports from Neenah and Menasha were particularly heartening. A succession of reports from the Industrial Commission's field representative, Alfred E. Poe, throughout 1936 pointed out that poor relief was very manageable. On June 29, 1936, Poe observed that of the $25,000 appropriated for poor relief, Neenah still had a positive balance and that it was unlikely it would excessively exceed its allocation by year's end, adding that the "city of Neenah is well able to carry its load." Menasha at this point was running a deficit in its $15,000 annual appropriation but Poe was not particularly alarmed at this trend, suggesting that the city might have "to secure some funds from some other source."[6]

If the county's twin cities appeared to be on the mend, the same could not be said for the City of Oshkosh. Poe reported that the current case load in June 1936 was 618, marking only a minor decrease from figures posted at the same time the previous year. When Poe discussed this matter with Mayor Weichering, his honor, "seemed to be rather pessimistic," prompted it would seem by the mayor's concern that the WPA was unlikely to offset demand for relief. Oshkosh's relief appropriation, a hefty $150,000, was nearly exhausted and was projected to turn a deficit on July 20. The city's intention to provide auxiliary funds was thwarted by an inability to reissue city bonds, leading Poe to speculate that the "city is faced with a rather serious financial situation."[7]

On April 7, 1937, on the threshold of a downward national trend in the economy and a rash of labor strikes in the City of Oshkosh, Representative Poe alerted his superiors that a rise in relief cases within the county controverted all of the other positive economic factors. The Neenah-Menasha Relief Group (these two cities had opted for a relief administration separate and apart from the City of Oshkosh) reported an increase in relief cases from 122 in October 1936 to 243 in February 1937. Poe contended that Neenah and Menasha were now feeling the pangs of suffering due to the influx of PWA workers brought in from other parts of the state suddenly finding it necessary to apply for relief. Oshkosh's figures, historically substantial, escalated from 583 in October 1936 to 777 at the time of Poe's report. In a later report on May 4, 1937 Poe made an unenviable comparison between the moderate plight of Neenah-Menasha as compared to its neighbor to the south. Oshkosh, Poe maintained, remained in a "lethargic condition," owing to the demise of the lumber industry. It was a city in a "decadent state that usually presages the general deterioration of a community...dependant upon one particular type of industrial activity." By contrast, Poe averred, Neenah-Menasha were aggressive, innovative communities with economies that by 1935 were not longer plagued by trouble.[8] In fact, as early as 1934, the twin cities had objected to being lumped together in a single administrative unit with the rest of Winnebago County, charging that Neenah and Menasha were compelled to shoulder costs generated by the City of Oshkosh. Neenah's mayor, William S. Campbell complained that the "city of Neenah through efficient government, has been able, and is able to continue to care for its poor, and that the adoption of the county unit plan would place an additional and unfair burden on the city." The agitation paid off, for in January 1935, Neenah and Menasha formed its own distinct relief unit, although the arrangement was derailed in March 1936.[9]

A combination of wishful thinking that the federal work relief programs (WPA) had helped revive the sagging economy and the pressure from conservative voices that the federal government was creating a monstrous welfare state led to a curtailment of WPA projects in early 1937.[10] By the middle of 1937, the chimerical recovery was exposed for what it was and the economy slid into another chasm, frequently referred to as the "Roosevelt Depression." Although local officials were aware of the potential impact cutbacks in WPA programs might have on relief challenges, enough projects were still in progress throughout 1937 and 1939 that the effect was mitigated somewhat before the federal government returned to deficit spending as a way of staunching the economic wounds. Between 1937 and 1938 many WPA projects throughout the county were either completed or in the process of completion. Each municipality within Winnebago County could proudly point to a variety of general infrastructure and aesthetic benefits, courtesy of federal largesse.

Rural Winneconne, for instance, had celebrated the completion of a brand new draw bridge spanning the Wolf River. Braving a roaring northwest wind, Winneconne citizens paraded down to the river and triumphantly crossed the new bridge on November 25, 1935. The bridge afforded a much faster and direct route east of town, as the only previous path entailed going south of the village to Omro, bypassing Lakes Poygan and Butte des Morts before heading to destinations eastward. The bridge did not come without some sacrifice. During the course of construction two workers slipped and fell to their deaths beneath the span. In 1938 J. W. Meigher, president of the village of Winneconne, announced that he had received the necessary WPA grant to enable the building and installation of a sanitary sewer system and disposal plant in the village. The project would employ around 100 men and the federal award would pay for nearly 70% of costs. Work on this project was completed in 1939.[11]

Both Neenah and Menasha had benefited enormously from federal assistance as well. Neenah's WPA awards went towards projects, while not exactly bedazzling in nature, were substantive in scope and result. Intercepting sewer lines were installed that separated water from catch basins and sanitary sewers. Nearly three miles of sewers were laid. A substantial amount of money was put into major curb and gutter construction and the concrete resurfacing of major streets in the city. A third project completed in 1937 was the construction of a major drainage ditch along an important artery into Neenah. And a final project saw the shoring up of the shoreline in Riverside Park. Neenah's relatively low relief case load and stable employment had enabled the city to escape most of the ravages of the depression, enough so, that in 1937 the city was able to finance with little outside assistance a new municipal water softening and filtering plant. While some men on relief received employment, the city foot the $115,540 bill all on its own.[12]

But it was Menasha's resolute pursuit of grant money that paid the greatest dividends. Like Neenah, Menasha shared in the upgrade to sewer systems, particularly in the area of Brighton Beach. However, it was the construction of a modern high school and a new sports complex, complete with a splendid grandstand, that Menasha boasted most about by the end of the decade. Apparently, the city council's somewhat spurious claim to a rise in juvenile delinquency helped secure the necessary funds for the latter project.[13]

The City of Oshkosh was not outdone by any other jurisdiction within the county, and it was remarkably successful in obtaining funds for a plethora of highway, sewer, environmental and infrastructure improvements. But the most significant project of all during the era of WPA projects belonged to the county at large--the construction of an entirely new courthouse complex. Even before the great economic collapse of 1929, complaints about the general inadequacy of the county's old courthouse building had been in circulation. Some thought the building antiquated in its public facilities. Lawyers were disenchanted with the limited number of chamber rooms in the old building and derided them as insufficient to handle the legal volume of the county. Some claimed the roof leaked. The minutes of the county's Board of Supervisors were peppered with proposals to build a new facility but with the emergence of the depression those ideas had to be shelved. All this changed with appearance of the WPA and PWA. In theory, the WPA of 1935 managed construction projects whose total costs did not exceed $25,000 whereas the PWA would handle major projects exceeding that price. In 1935 the County Board chairman appointed a committee of supervisors to discover in what ways the county could reap the bounty of federal dollars. Topping the list was the recommendation that a new courthouse be built.[14]

Work on the new county courthouse began in late 1936. For the next two years a massive workforce toiled endlessly to complete the million dollar edifice. When the building was dedicated on July 27, 1938 the public marveled at the majestic exterior and the stunning interior. According to one admirer, the county courthouse held the "honor of being one of the finest courthouses in the Middle West."[15] Ironically, administrative wrangling within the Roosevelt administration led to the canceling of PWA assistance. Consequently, the county and the City of Oshkosh were compelled to meet the costs which the city did by tapping into municipal savings. All the same, federal tax dollars allowed the county to use WPA workers to demolish the old courthouse building, salvaging anything of value. Much of the retrieved material went into the construction of other buildings, including a municipal garage on the west side of the south ramp leading up to the upper level of the city's incinerator plant.[16]

The programs of the New Deal, especially the WPA, were not just about bricks and mortar or relief and employment. By 1937 they had become virtually ensconced in the very culture of the county. The projects and the protocols surrounding them became part and parcel of the daily fabric of life during the latter part of the Thirties. People in the county continued to live their lives day in and day out but the rhythm of their existence was indelibly marked by the culture of the New Deal. Neenah resident, Finley F. Martin, insistent that others of his generation were in agreement with him, thought that living was better during the depression than at any other time. "Things were cheap, things were easy going," he maintained, and "you didn't worry about what was going to happen...it was a pleasant time to live." While admitting that there "were some people on relief," this citizen insisted that "you had the WPA and all those alphabetical work projects...I just had the feeling that things had slowed down and you didn't feel the pressure." Another Neenah resident, Oliver M. Thomsen, took conspicuous pride in his Lutheran congregation for nary one of them were on the dole. "Sometimes they were a little tight," he admitted, "but they made it...they were all taking care of their own needs." With apparent satisfaction, he recalled an elderly lady and congregant in the west side of Neenah whom everyone mistakenly thought a son was supporting. When they discovered otherwise, the congregation saw to it very quickly that she was taken off of welfare. "She had to have help," Thomsen conceded, "but she got it from the church instead of the public."[17]

For some, like Genevieve Schierl of Menasha, little had been altered by the coming of hard times. She recalled with evident fondness that women used to head to downtown Menasha where you could obtain anything you wanted from the grocery stores there. "In those days you'd take your baby buggies and go to downtown in the afternoon," she explained, "to pick up your groceries for dinner that night...it seemed to be kind of a ritual." In Oshkosh, Clarence Jungwirth, a teenager during the Depression, recalled that most people made do with the simpler pleasures of life. Many unemployed in the city congregated and formed unofficial social clubs. Since automobiles were in short supply, they used unoccupied garages, propped up a card table with chairs, gathered around the ubiquitous radio that provided news, music or sporting events to while away the time. If enough money was pooled, the members arranged for a keg of beer or a case of soda to make the meetings more sociable and convivial. Adults and teenagers played cards, particularly during the winter. Jungwirth attributed the popularity of these games as a way of keeping adolescents out of trouble. Summertime brought people outside. With few cars available and little disposable income, people took to the streets. They attended baseball games in the city parks or gathered with friends on street corners or front porches to shoot the breeze.[18]

"Typical family life changed," notes one student of the depression in Oshkosh. Visits to movie houses became less frequent and families relied on credit from local grocers to put dinner on the table. People did cheap things; they played cards, watched amateur sports, and did more than their fair share of hunting and fishing since these amusements carried the added bonus of securing free victuals. Again, the radio enjoyed booming popularity during this era. Jack Benny, Fred Allen, Ed Wynn and a host of others became familiar household mainstays. Kids were thrilled by the adventures of the likes of the *Lone Ranger*, the *Green Hornet* and the *Shadow*. Oshkosh during this time became home to a professional basketball team. Lonnie Darling, a local Oshkosh businessman, procured enough money to start a franchise for the city. Known as the Oshkosh All Stars the team won the National Basketball League's championship in 1942. Soon afterwards, however, larger cities with wealthier backers started to flex their corporate muscle and the days of professional basketball in Oshkosh came to an inglorious end. Like Jungwirth, James I. Metz concluded that the Depression for those who could remember it was not all gloom and despair. "There were rough times," Metz acknowledged, "but they were simpler times."[19]

For young adults there were more titillating amusements. A new ten-story hotel, rivaling the older, more established Atheneum, was built by Conrad Raulf and opened for business in 1928, perhaps, a case of poor timing. An impressive ballroom dominated the second floor. Every Thursday afternoon and evening during the Thirties the ballroom featured the Raulf's weekly "Walkathon." According to one former resident of Oshkosh some twenty to thirty housemaids used their weekly afternoons off and marched to the Raulf in hopes of meeting a similar number of unemployed young men for the privilege of walking around the dance floor "until either their feet went numb or they dropped from exhaustion." The last standing couple came away with the then princely sum of twenty-five cents a head. The event also drew upon the attendance of young men on leave from nearby CCC camps, plainly evident in their rough olive-drab army uniforms.[20]

John Livingstone, a young but perceptive observer of Oshkosh during the Great Depression, noted how much the WPA had become ingrained into the culture of the late Thirties. Living near city hall, he can vividly recall how with remarkable precision unemployed workers drove their model-A Fords to city hall to pick up their relief checks every week. An aspiring violinist, Livingstone appreciated the funds supplied by the WPA which helped breathe "new life into despondent artists, musicians and thespians by providing them with places to practice their art with subsistence incomes." On September 30, 1937 the *Oshkosh Northwestern* reported that the attendance record at the WPA recreation center had again been shattered the previous evening when the WPA concert orchestra presented a free program along with a new drama acted by the WPA Drama players. A week later the recreation center announced plans for a very busy schedule of organized sports and classes in tin craft and weaving. The WPA also loaned books, toys and bicycles to those who otherwise would have done without.[21]

Nearby Livingstone's home on Central Avenue the WPA had assumed ownership of a rundown old mansion and created a "social club" setting for unemployed men. The first floor was taken over by those who wished to play cards or cribbage. The upstairs was given over to a potpourri of organized events or instruction. In one case, as Livingstone recalled, "a tiny British septuagenarian, Mr. Ryder, replete with pince-nez glasses, gave free instruction in fencing." As Livingstone's father's income was steady, it normally prohibited the family access to relief and its corollary benefits. Young John, fearful he would be barred from fencing lessons, raced home, put on his "oldest, shabbiest clothes," and returned to the clubhouse determined to fit the bill.[22]

One of the things the WPA could not postpone was an eventual showdown between workers and their employers in Winnebago County. The last three years of the Thirties witnessed a rash of disputes between labor and capital that evolved into bitter strikes. The reasons for this outbreak were both numerous and complex. Long-postponed labor demands resurfaced at a point when the national and local economy appeared to be on the mend. Union recognition by owners, better wages, shorter hours, and improved working conditions topped the list of concerns. Accelerating this looming conflict between labor and capital was the passage in July 1935 of the National Labor Relations Act (NLRA), more commonly known as the Wagner Act. This law supported the rights of labor in the private sector to organize their own unions, to engage in collective bargaining, and, most importantly, to participate in strikes and other forms of coercive activity in support of their demands. Federal arbitration in labor disputes would be provided by the powerful National Labor Relations Board (NLRB). The nub of the matter, however, was that many employers refused to recognize the Wagner Act as law. In the first two years following the passage of the bill, several appellate courts struck down enforcement of the act on the grounds of its unconstitutionality. Moreover, many labor organizations neglected to exploit the law or use the NLRB to their advantage, preferring instead, to engage in a series of sit down strikes which only escalated conflict.[23]

That Winnebago County would be swept up in the tide of labor disputes after 1935 should come as little surprise. Almost every industrial center in the United States was affected by struggles, often violent, between employers and workers. By 1937, strikes had paralyzed the steel industry from Chicago to Cleveland, Toledo to Youngstown and on to Johnstown, Pennsylvania. At the Republic Steel plant in Chicago, policemen waded into a gathering of peaceful strikers, bashing anyone they could lay their hands on, killing several protestors in the process. Eight were killed in Monroe, Michigan when some of the workers attempted to return to work. Reports of strike violence were splashed all over the pages of the *Oshkosh Northwestern*, and they were so numerous that it featured a column headlined, "Strikes at a Glance" for several weeks in the middle of 1937. The conservative paper felt compelled to observe in one of its editorials that the violence was bound to "damage the labor cause and welfare," and that it was not fair to "credit all labor troubles to the recalcitrance of the employers."[24]

During the height of the national turmoil labor unrest settled into Winnebago County. But, again, like in so many other matters like relief needs and unemployment factors, labor disturbances did not occur in any uniform manner throughout the county; Oshkosh, more than any other place, experienced problems to a much greater degree than elsewhere. Workers in the paper industries of Neenah and Menasha had enjoyed relatively secure employment throughout the depression years and apparently enjoyed a cooperative relationship with management and capital. By contrast, Oshkosh's workers had suffered dreadfully during the depression and harbored bitter memories of labor disputes in the woodworking mills going back to the great strike of 1898. The animosity between workers and owners in the Sawdust City would make the relationship between Shakespeare's Montagues and Capulets seem positively cordial.

There had been a couple of strikes in the twin cities before 1937. A small-scale strike at the International Wire Works in 1931 had been broken by the introduction of non-union workers and a brief work stoppage at Menasha Wooden Ware, as previously discussed, had been resolved by arbitration. But in 1937, the year of strikes, a degree of labor unrest took root. Several workers at the construction site of the new Menasha High School went on strike demanding a closed shop for skilled and unskilled labor, higher wages, and a more favorable work schedule. They received a wage increase but nothing else. Workers at two retail lumber facilities, the Durham and Lieber companies, went on strike in late April. Supported by company truck drivers and volunteer pickets from Oshkosh, the two-month strike won several impressive concessions from ownership, including union recognition, adjusted work schedules, and an increase in pay.[25]

Whereas these two incidents were relatively miniscule and isolated, labor unrest later that year at the region's largest employer, Kimberly-Clark, had the potential of being explosive. Problems arose, somewhat ironically, soon after the company had come to contractual terms with the recognized workers' union, the Employee's Independent Union. The one-year contract established working schedules, hourly wages, and a closed labor shop. One month into the contract, however, both workers and management declared it null and void. Rival unions, the International Brotherhood of Pulp Makers and the International Brotherhood of Pulp, Sulphite and Paper Millworkers accused Kimberly-Clark of illegally imposing a closed shop and several other violations of the Wagner Act. The NLRB agreed to labor's claims in virtually every indictment. Further chaos was deflected when management made overt efforts to come to terms. Company representative, S. F. Shattuck, launched a saturated media blitz in the *Neenah Daily News-Times*. A series of five articles outlined that the company's policy was to recognize whatever organization workers chose. Shattuck also successfully appealed to paternal instincts, citing that Kimberly-Clark had always fostered a climate of good employee management relations. Thereafter, employee belligerence tapered off, and labor rebuffed the offers of any outside attempts to organize. In late 1938 the NLRB recognized two separate unions for two different kinds of employees within the company as the sole bargaining agents for the workers. Not until 1943 did an AFL union supplant this arrangement at Kimberly-Clark.[26]

All the same, the Twin Cities' labor problems paled in comparison to Oshkosh. It seemed for a while during the late Thirties that the only industrial facilities not on strike at least once were those that struck twice. The list of striking employees by craft or trade included mill, furniture, luggage and trunks, clothing and match stick makers. The Leach Company, a heavy machinery firm and Wisconsin Axle, soon to be the city's largest employer, were both affected by strikes during this period. Rounding out the list were butchers, glass-makers, hotel employees and dairy and creamery workers. But the most notable strikes involved the Sawdust City's traditional industry--the wood mills and furniture plants. With virtually no advance notice over 1,400 millworkers walked out of their jobs on the evening of April 29, 1937. Five sash and door outfits, the Morgan, Mc Millen, Radford, Foster-Lothman, and Oshkosh Millwork, were stunned by the stoppage in the first major strike in this industry since 1898. The strike was called by the American Federation of Labor (AFL) and Millmen's Local, No. 1363. The night before laborers had gathered at the Oshkosh Recreational Auditorium, and although the ballots were cast in secret, reports indicated the vote as 1,238 to 35 to proceed with a strike. All of the affected plants were immediately picketed and union officials pledged that 1,300 to 1,400 strikers would begin around-the-clock picket shifts, each of which were slated for six hours. Contracts submitted by union officials called for a 40 hour and 5 day work week, a minimum of 50 to 67 ½ cent hourly wage, time and a half for overtime and double time for holiday work. This contrasted with the present range of 30-50 cents an hour, a minimum 45-hour per week work schedule, and no significant bonuses for overtime or holiday work. According to Bertrand A. Philipp, president of the millmen's organization, employers had countered with a measly raise of 5 cents an hour. By the morning of April 30 all work at the five plants had come to an end and nothing was coming out of them. A visit by a reporter from the *Oshkosh Northwestern* evinced news that pickets were unevenly distributed at various plants but that all of them were peaceful. At the Mc Millen plant, for instance, several of the strikers played baseball and drank free milk donated by a friendly supporter. At the Foster-Lothman operation millworkers jovially suggested that photographs be taken to commemorate the event.[27]

Strike momentum surged on May 4 when nearly 400 employees at four furniture plants, Banderob, Buckstaff, Badger Lumber and Freeman Furniture, staged a walkout. Like the millworkers, employees at these sites wanted a closed shop, standard wage scale with a minimum of 40 cents and a maximum of 60 cents per hour, a 40-hour work week and time and incentive pay for overtime and holiday work. Management's initial response fell short of the wage increases sought and established a 50-hour work week during peak seasons. As in the case of the millworker's strike, picket lines were to be maintained around the clock.[28]

Hopes that labor unrest might get settled were buoyed on May 15 when 90 workers of the Oshkosh Millwork Company reconciled with management and promised to return to work pending an official settlement. At this point no details of the terms were made available, but it was hoped that this agreement might become the template for the remaining three millwork firms and the furniture plants as well. By this point, John D. Spencer, relief director in Oshkosh, was denying worker applications for assistance. A delegation of roughly ten workers called on Mayor Weichering's office to demand his intervention on their behalf.[29]

The disruption these strikes had upon the economic stability of the city of Oshkosh drove many community leaders, including the mayor, into profound despair. On May 18, Weichering addressed owners and strikers in a public message published in the *Oshkosh Northwestern*, urging them to settle their differences so that industries might resume operation and supply needed employment. Referring to the preliminary settlement at the Oshkosh Millwork Company, where workers "were protecting their jobs...and helping employers meet [their] obligations," the mayor plaintively inquired, "Why can't all the factories work while adjusting this strike situation?" The matter was quite simple, or, so the mayor thought. "We want fair wages paid in Oshkosh and it's up to employers to pay them and the men to accept them and go to work. That is the real issue."[30]

A month into the millworker's strike, the owners of the four stricken mills purchased a large two-page spread in the *Oshkosh Northwestern*, with the banner headline, "A Plain Statement to Employees and the Public," outlining their respective positions on the issues involved in the current strike. They first wanted to establish that their financial standings were nowhere as positive as the public seemed to be assuming. The statement went on to detail the concessions to workers that they were willing to offer, particularly in modest wage increases and reduced working hours, but were clear that wage hikes being demanded by the union exceeded the total combined net profit margin of all the owners for the year 1936, and "based upon the present business outlook will no doubt exceed the combined net profit of the employers for the year 1937."[31]

Workers and union representatives were unfazed both by the owner's revelations or their logic. They fortified their resolve and encouraged solidarity in the face of unemployment going into its sixth week. Union organizers promoted a parade, soon to be dubbed, "Win the Strike," through the streets of Oshkosh on the evening of June 4. In what was described as the "greatest peaceable labor demonstration in the history of Oshkosh," nearly 3500 supporters paraded down Main Street and over the bridge into the south side, disbanding finally at South Park where the typical speeches were made to a gathering of nearly 8,000. Armed with legal assurances, keynote speaker, Andrew J. Biemiller, a Milwaukee assemblyman, vowed that the strike would go on to ultimate victory, and warned that if "employers interfere with labor organization today, they may be in danger of changing their fine clothes for suits with little black stripes."[32]

Worker resolve and owner intransigence forced an exasperated Mayor Weichering to cable a telegram to Governor La Follette requesting the services of the state's Labor Relations Board.

Since he believed that the Oshkosh mill strike was "not getting anywhere," and in fact, was a major retrograde movement for the city, Weichering was convinced that outside intervention was necessary at this point. Curiously, it was on the same date, June 11, that the telegram was sent that word was circulating that the Badger Company and its employees were making considerable progress towards resolving their differences. Such rumors proved a bit premature. On the 15th of June, workers at the Badger Company voted 115 to 2 to reject the latest offer made by the mill company, and the report that some of the workers at the Freeman Furniture factory had agreed to work likewise proved unfounded. As for Mayor Weichering's hopes for outside arbitration, no members of the Labor Board were reported to have arrived in the city, although the invitation had been sent a full week earlier.[33]

Something mystical must have occurred between June 18 when workers at Badger Lumber and Freeman Furniture rejected management's latest offer and the next day when it was announced that these two operations would resume business the following Monday. Although official terms were not announced at the time, they were ostensibly "satisfactory to both parties." The strike in the city's mills and furniture plants that had quickly surfaced in early May abruptly ended by the beginning of July. On June 21, 140 employees at the Buckstaff Company voted to accept the terms offered. By this time, two members of the Labor Board, Voyta Wrabetz and the Reverend Francis J. Haas, had arrived in Oshkosh and quickly arranged conferences with the representatives of the Millmen's local union. Although they did not have powers of binding arbitration, they were likely persuasive, since it was announced on June 25 that "distinct progress" towards a settlement was being made. Nonetheless, the Millmen's local No. 1363 gathered in the Recreational Auditorium and quickly rejected the terms that employers had agreed to as suggested by the Labor Board. This unexpected outcome threw the near-apoplectic Mayor Weichering into another round of fretting. "What is to become of Oshkosh?" the mayor moaned in a statement made to the *Oshkosh Northwestern*. Believing that the woodworker's strike should have been only about increased wages, he deplored that worker insistence on a closed shop sabotaged the most recent round of negotiations. The pathos continued when he inquired if there were ten public-spirited citizens who would come to his office and sit down and resolve the current problem. "A solution must be found," he demanded, "that will answer this crisis...one that will leave our mills in a position to compete and also give our workmen a wage where they can live comfortably." And he ended his epistle rather forlornly with the plea, "Will you men of Oshkosh help?"[34]

The fear that was beginning to grip Oshkosh was on its way to being dispelled when members of the bargaining unit for employees at the Radford Mill accepted on July 9 the latest offer from the company by a margin of 12 to 1. Pay scales were established that were remarkably close to employee demands at the beginning of the strike. A 45-hour work week was accepted, and although no explicit employer acceptance of a closed shop was mentioned, the fact that the company had dealt exclusively with the local millworker's union appeared to be *de facto* compliance. The following day, workers at the McMillen plant followed suit and accepted an offer from company officials reported to be remarkably similar to that accepted the day before by Radford employees. The *Oshkosh Northwestern* hailed these two agreements as, "Joyous News for Oshkosh!" Although there had been murmurs that employees at the Morgan Company would not accept agreements along the lines that Radford and Mc Millen workers had, the Morgan strike came to an end on July 13 when workers by a 25 to 1 margin came to terms. Workers at the Foster-Lothman plant held out a bit longer but within a week workers there were reporting to work. With the resolution of the millworker's strikes the remaining two furniture plants on strike, Buckstaff and Badger Lumber, resumed operations in short order.[35]

With the resolutions of these strikes, it appeared as though most of Oshkosh had returned to work. But this idyllic portrait of owner-employee cooperation was marred by the emergence and continuance of another strike at the Wisconsin Match Company. No sooner were the mill strikes drawing to a close when employees at this plant walked out on July 7. Although smaller in scale, this was the city's most protracted and bitter of strikes. Whereas pickets at the mills boasted of their non-violent resistance, including taking group photos, listening to orchestral music, and lapping up ice cream, strikers and strike leaders for match workers were decidedly more defiant and bellicose in their approach towards management and owners at the match plant.

Although the match workers, some 275 of them, at the Wisconsin Match Company shared some of the same grievances as their comrades in the mill and furniture industry, there were several important logistical and exceptional issues that placed them in a different bargaining position throughout the summer and fall of 1937. First of all, the Wisconsin Match Company was a subsidiary of a national corporation, the Diamond Match Company, with headquarters located in New York. Negotiations, then, proved more difficult because local executives were relatively powerless in dealing directly with labor representatives, as they required approval in most contractual matters from corporate headquarters. There were also safety issues at the match plant unique to this industry, such as the need for round-the-clock firemen to deal with the possibility of explosive fires. Employees at the match plant and their union representatives also were convinced that the parent company had been enjoying unprecedented profits over the last two years of recovery and that labor demands for better wages and shorter hours could no longer be brushed aside by the groans of owners that workers should be grateful they had jobs at all.

The first stirrings of trouble at the Wisconsin Match Company were revealed in a telegram sent by Francis B. Gerhart, President of the National Match Workers Council, when he cabled the President of the AFL, William Green, that the management of the corporation had refused to sit down with representatives of the Federal Labor Board even to discuss matters at the Oshkosh plant. Preliminary discussions between Wisconsin Match and Gerhart set the tone for the looming strike when at one point, Mayor Weichering, concerned what a strike might mean for the safety of the plant, threatened to jail Gerhart if he interfered with any measures he might take to insure safe conditions. When discussions continued to languish between management and labor, 275 men and women decided to walk off the job on the very day that Radford and Mc Millen workers were beginning the trek back to work. Picket lines were formed at 4:30 a.m. on July 12 around the match factory under a strike order called by the United Match Workers Local No. 20385, an AFL affiliate. The pickets barred all entry into the plant, including Franklin Moore, vice-president and general manager of the plant, as well as members of the office staff.[36]

According to August Tiedje, president of the local union, the workers demanded increased wages, recognition of the union as the bargaining agent for all employees, and the right to deal with an authorized representative of the owners. Countering union demands, Franklin Moore stated that the company had provided steady employment for the last six years at wage levels above the average for the community of Oshkosh. Tiedje countered without acknowledging the veracity of Moore's claims but seemed to infer that wages at the match plant were no longer competitive with those won by the local millworkers in the recent strikes. Moore charged that strikers who had hustled themselves out of the plant in the early hours of July 12 left it in a dangerous condition by extinguishing fires under the boilers and abandoning the plant without inside fire protection and no watchmen. Since inflammatory materials were stored at the factory, he requested to station a fireman and watchman as a safety measure. Whereas both sides expressed the hope that violence could be averted, an impasse had been reached and negotiations were temporarily broken off.[37]

In a lengthy report to William Green, David Sigman, Organizer for the AFL, confirmed the dismal prospects for a speedy resolution to the match worker's strike in Oshkosh. While he hoped that both management and labor would agree to binding arbitration over the matter of wage increases, he believed that the owners were likely to be very obstinate in their deliberations. The hard line adopted by the Diamond Match Company was matched by the local union. For several weeks in August negotiations resumed only to break off, despite the best efforts of the NLRB, the AFL conciliation team, and the mayor of Oshkosh to broker a successful agreement.[38]

At one point in late August the strike at Wisconsin Match assumed ominous tones, only to end up as one of the more colorful, even farcical, episodes of the long strike. Franklin Moore had on several occasions approached Mayor Weichering with requests to enter the plant along with a cadre of clerical workers to attend to administrative tasks, including the distribution of the last payroll dating back to the beginning of the strike on July 12. Pickets had earlier denied Moore access to the plant. Weichering responded that he thought it only fair that Moore have the right to enter the plant. "It would be different," the mayor reasoned, "if the company wanted to go in and make matches." Informed of the mayor's position, local union leader, August Tiedje, defiantly postured that if the company was going to use such methods, then, "we're going to use different tactics, too." The strikers' determination gave pause to the mayor to reflect about the situation, concerned, now, that using police force to break a picket line might be inviting violence and anarchy.[39]

The mayor's indecision and timidity were suddenly reversed when, on September 2, he announced that company officials would receive police protection in gaining access to the plant and asked union officials to restrain pickets from making any attempt to block entry. The request fell on deaf ears. On the fourth of September, policemen, with Chief Gabbert on point, formed a "flying wedge" and pushed aside a group of pickets, chiefly women strikers, and finally overwhelmed the last line of defense assembled in front of the plant's door. Strikers had armed themselves with sticks, bricks and clubs but eschewed employing them in the fracas. One of the strikers, Elsie Cornell, was reportedly brushed off her feet and was carried away, having fainted in the rush led by Chief Gabbert. Two other women strikers, Frieda Kunde and Anna Jungbauer, were placed in a patrol wagon, driven around the corner and then promptly released. Strikers leveled jeers and catcalls against the police for their tactics and the resounding epithet, "scabs" was directed at the clerical staff that had been escorted into the plant. When the affair entered its final stages, the call went up to march on city hall to confront the mayor for his sordid role in the day's work. Several dozen strikers went off in that direction, armed with throaty voices and vulgar slogans but largely dispersed before arriving at their intended destination. What could have ended up as a very bloody battle emerged as no more than a tempest in a teapot.[40]

The strike at Wisconsin Match inexorably rolled into the fall of 1937. By this time striking workers remained firm in their resolve to win the strike but many of the rank and file were feeling the pinch of two-months' unemployment. This was reflected in Tiedje's importuning the national labor union of match workers to provide sustenance. Noting the justness of the cause, Tiejde appealed to "sister unions and individual members as the one hope against being victimized by a huge monopoly." Francis Gerhart investigated the possibility of a sympathy strike at the other plants within the Diamond Match Company, as well as these workers donating part of their dues for a relief fund for the Oshkosh strikers. Unfortunately, little became of these schemes. Moreover, since the local union in Oshkosh had not been in formation for a full year in September 1937, its members were not automatically entitled to strike benefits.[41] The precarious financial situation was echoed again by Gerhart in his report to AFL chief, William Green, on October 5, 1937. Referring to the local Oshkosh union, Gerhart pleaded for financial assistance as all means of raising funds locally had been exhausted and that they were, in fact, flat broke. He warned that the fight in Oshkosh was of paramount importance as a litmus test because the Diamond Match Company was resolutely embarking upon a scheme to undermine all unions among match workers. "If these workers are left by themselves," he argued, "you can rest assured that they will take a licking from their employer." Strangely, however, it was the Diamond Match Company which blinked first. In early October corporate headquarters sent a representative to Oshkosh and it resulted in a tentative agreement being reached. An exuberant Gerhart cabled Green on October 16 that the strike had been settled, that the company offered a 4 cent per hour wage increase and that 95% of the union voted to accept.[42]

Despite this apparent resolution, employees were not convinced the company was faithful in its implementation of the terms of agreement. In fact, Gerhart had to inform Green in January 1938 that the local union had taken the strike vote because of dissatisfaction with the good faith of management. David Sigman of the AFL was dispatched by Green to Oshkosh to handle the next round of negotiations. It took a revised agreement between management and employees in September 1938 to finally bring to a close the match worker dispute. With that agreement relative labor peace descended upon Winnebago County.[43]

Notes

1. Department of Commerce, *Census of Manufactures, 1935, (Washington, D.C)*, as reported in the *Oshkosh Northwestern*, April 16, 1917.
2. *Oshkosh Northwestern*, January 19, 1937; Steven B. Karges, *Neenah-Menasha Wisconsin and the Great Depression*. M.A. Thesis, University of Wisconsin, Madison, 1965), p. 105.
3. U.S. Department of Commerce, *Census of Manufactures, 1935*, as reported in the *Oshkosh Northwestern*, April 16, 1937.
4. *Oshkosh Northwestern*, April 16, 1917.
5. *Oshkosh Northwestern*, August 26 and September 15, 1937. See also, Steve R. Lankau, *A Thumbnail Sketch of Former City of Oshkosh Industrial Firms*, p. 82.
6. UWO-ARC, *Public Welfare Department Field Report of Alfred E. Poe, June 29, 1936* in County Administrative File, 1932-1967, Series 1406, Box No. 128, Folder: 70-0a, Winnebago County Summary Field Reports. In July 1937 both Neenah and Menasha's relief costs indicated substantial declines from the previous year's report. See *Oshkosh Northwestern*, August 5, 1937.
7. UWO-ARC, *Public Welfare Department Field Report of Alfred E. Poe, June 29, 1936* in County Administrative File, 1932-1967, Series 1406, Box No. 128, Folder 70-0a, Winnebago County Summary Field Reports.
8. UWO-ARC, *Public Welfare Department Field Report of Alfred E. Poe, May 4, 1937* in County Administrative File, 1932-1967, Series 1406, Box No. 128, Folder 70-0a, Winnebago County Summary Field Reports.
9. Campbell quoted in Steven B. Karges, *Neenah-Menasha Wisconsin and the Great Depression, p. 81.*
10. The conservative-leaning *Oshkosh Northwestern* reflected the growing criticism of New Deal programs. In an editorial on June 3, 1937, the paper wailed that the WPA was a stop-gap measure, and it was "never intended to provide opportunities for permanent careers...or federal sinecures." And those "who are devoid of any ambition to earn a living in private employment because they feel that they have established permanent connections with governmental largesse will have to be disillusioned, sooner or later."

11. *Oshkosh Northwestern*, November 25, 1935. Announcement of the federal grant for the sanitary system was made in the *Winneconne Times*, March 17, 1938.
12. Steven B. Karges,*Neenah-Menasha Wisconsin and the Great Depression*, pp. 97-98.
13. A second justification for the building of a grandstand was based on the proposal's claim that "citizens of Menasha are very enthusiastic sportsmen...". See SHSW, *Federal Records, Works Projects Administration, Wisconsin Division,* WPA Project Card Files, 1936-1942. Series 1688, Box No. 5, Folder: Menasha, Project Series No. 2D-1487.
14. Charles D. Goff and Martin Gruberg, *A History of Winnebago County Government* (Oshkosh: Dr. Martin Gruberg, 1998), p. 55.
15. John W. Miner, "Two Decades of Oshkosh Progress, Despite Odds," in *Wisconsin Magazine* (Oshkosh Edition). (Appleton: Madison Publishing Co., December 1950), p. 4.
16. Steve R. Langkau, *A History of the City of Oshkosh Sanitation Department*, p. 17.
17. Recollections of Finley F. Martin and Oliver M. Thomsen, in Michael O'Brien, *Neenah-Menasha: An Oral History,* pp.14-16.
18. Recollections of Genevieve Schierl in Michael O'Brien, *Neenah-Menasha: An Oral History*, p. 15. The memories of Clarence Jungwirth, a local historian and author, can be found in *Magazine of the Oshkosh Public Museum.* Vol. 13, No. 2, (Summer. 2001), pp. 1-4.
19. James I. Metz, *Foundations to Remember: Reflections upon Oshkosh's 150 Years*, pp. 29-31.
20. John Livingstone, *The Importance of Being from Oshkosh,* pp. 17-18.
21. John Livingstone, *The Importance of Being from Oshkosh,* pp. 17-18; *Oshkosh Northwestern*, September 30 and October 6, 1937.
22. John Livingstone, *The Importance of Being from Oshkosh,* p. 18.
23. A very concise description of the NLRA can be found in Wikipedia, http://en.wikepedea.org/wiki/National_Labor_Relations_Act.
24. *Oshkosh Northwestern*, June 14, 1937.
25. Steven B. Karges, *Neenah-Menasha Wisconsin and the Great Depression*, pp. 107-08; *Oshkosh Northwestern,* June 5, 1937.
26. S. Karges, *Neenah-Menasha Wisconsin and the Great Depression,* pp. 109-11.
27. *Oshkosh Northwestern*, April 30, 1937. Note the Paine Lumber Company was still in the process of retooling for a start up later in the year, so, it was not affected by the strike.
28. *Oshkosh Northwestern*, May 4, 1937. At about this same time, approximately 100 workers at the Leach Company, located on South Main Street, went on strike as well. See *Oshkosh Northwestern,* May 16, 1937.
29. *Oshkosh Northwestern,* May 15, 1937.
30. Weichering's public address was published in the *Oshkosh Northwestern,* May 18, 1937.
31. *Oshkosh Northwestern,* May 29, 1937.
32. *Oshkosh Northwestern,* June 2, 4, and 5, 1937. It should be noted that the Banderob Company had come to terms with its employees on May 26.
33. All these proceedings were reported in the *Oshkosh Northwestern,* June 11, 15, and 18, 1937.
34. *Oshkosh Northwestern,* June 19, 21, 23, 25, 26, and 29, 1937. Two days after the mayor's appeal seven men had come forward and agreed to meet. A committee was organized and drafted a resolution to help end the strike since it was causing much hardship

to the community at large. This stance was seconded by the *Oshkosh Northwestern* editorial of July 8, 1937. See also *Oshkosh Northwestern*, July 1 and 7, 1937.
35. *Oshkosh Northwestern*, July 19, 12, and 13, 1937.
36. SHSW, Telegram from F.B. Gerhart to William Green, April 28, 1937 in *American Federation of Labor Papers: Strikes and Agreements File*. U.S. Mss. 117A/7, Box No. 37, Folder 20385; *Oshkosh Northwestern*, July 12 and 17, 1937.
37. *Oshkosh Northwestern*, July 25, 1937.
38. SHSW, David Sigman to William Green, August 3, 1937 in *American Federation of Labor Papers: Strikes and Agreements File*, U.S. Mss 117A/7, Box No. 37, Folder 20385.
39. *Oshkosh Northwestern*, August 26, 27, and 28, 1937.
40. All of the day's activities were reported in the *Oshkosh Northwestern*, September 2 and 4, 1937. The use of women in the front line of the demonstration was a tactic learned from the strike of 1898. Like then, Tiedje believed the police would hesitate before manhandling women.
41. SHSW, August Tiedje to The United Matchworkers' Federal Labor Union, received September 23, 1937 in *American Federation of Labor Papers: Strikes and Agreements File*, U.S. Mss. 117A/7, Box No. 37, Folder 20385.
42. SHSW, Francis Gerhart to William Green, October 5, 1937, and Telegram, Francis Gerhart to William Green, October 16, 1937 in *American Federation of Labor Papers: Strikes and Agreements File*, U.S. Mss. 117A/7, Box No. 37, Folder 20385.
43. SHSW, Francis Gerhart to William Green, January 22, 1938; Telegram,William Green to Francis Gerhart, January 24, 1938, and Labor Agreement, signed by Franklin Moore, August Tiedje and Roena Ulrich, dated August 26, 1938 in *American Federation of Labor Papers: Strikes and Agreements File*, U.S. Mss. 117A/7, Box No. 37, Folder 20385.

Epilogue

Hope on the Horizon

As it did for each of the nine years of the Great Depression, the *Oshkosh Northwestern* deigned to reflect on the passing of 1939 and to cast projections for the new year 1940. As usual, the end-of-year editorial was plastered with hackneyed, pious platitudes. The "national outlook [was] cheerful," an "inventory of goods and prospects" taken by business leaders, "appear to be in a hopeful and optimistic state of mind regarding the coming year," and so on and so on. Yet at the close of the Thirties Winnebago County was indeed poised on the threshold of better times; the decade of distress and despair was coming to an end. Improvements came gradually, and, as so often the case elsewhere, the wagon of war would help ride the county out of the Great Depression.[1]

As a new decade beckoned the county was still not out of the woods. Those engaged in agriculture and the dairy industry continued to be buffeted by the vagaries of supply and demand and ever-fluctuating prices. In Oshkosh nearly 2500 families remained eligible for food stamps. Relief cases remained both open and abundant. The woodworking mills, although back in business, were still reeling from reduction in demand and the tumult of labor troubles. According to one observer, "it would not be until 1963 that the number of employed people in the city reached the level of 1928." The lingering gravity of the depression's effects upon the people of Oshkosh might best be illustrated in a meeting of the city council in late 1939. When it was proposed that an available $600 be spread among some 90 municipal workers in the form of a raise, one alderman groused that "with all the people in this city that are looking for jobs, city employees are pretty well off." Only Neenah and Menasha rode out the storm of depression relatively unscathed. It would seem that the paper industry was indispensable and the general public remained rather partial to the various uses of tissue paper.[2]

The Great Depression also altered the economic landscape of the county. Admittedly, the paper industry of Neenah and Menasha proved virtually depression-proof. The paper mills continued to expand there and it was not until later in the century that considerable downsizing in this industry occurred. On the other hand, the depression wreaked havoc upon Oshkosh's exclusive reliance upon the woodworking industry. Although the mills survived the Thirties, they would never again be the lucrative businesses they had been on the eve of 1929. The coming of World War II, so often credited with ending the Great Depression, did not immediately stimulate the home-building sector. The north woods which had furnished the mills with their raw materials had been overly harvested and the post-war boom in the tourist industry made further logging unpopular. The Fifties introduced aluminum window and door frames, further eroding demand for Oshkosh's mills. Finally, labor costs were viewed as prohibitively high in Oshkosh, resulting in the establishment of new millworks in the deep South. As a consequence, the great woodworking mills which had lined the Fox River, and which had given the city its very nickname, "Sawdust City," had either entirely disappeared or reduced to such a diluted form as to be unrecognizable within three decades of the Great Depression.

The demise of the woodworking industry, which had caused so much suffering during the Great Depression, might have been a blessing in disguise for the city's economic health in that it encouraged diversification. The Paine Lumber Company had long enjoyed the status of the city's largest employer up to 1929. By 1940, Wisconsin Axle assumed this coveted position. In fact, the demands of war triggered an economic boom in the city, as industries like Wisconsin Axle, the Leach Company and Oshkosh Truck began grinding out the machines, components and weapons during the Forties. Wisconsin Axle, for example, received government contracts well in advance of the Japanese attack at Pearl Harbor to make vehicle axles and transmissions for tanks, amphibious craft and the like. Similarly, Oshkosh Truck would cash in on government contracts once hostilities with the Axis powers started in 1942. More importantly, however, these were industries that proved easily convertible to serve the requirements of a post-war building boom.[3]

The Great Depression came to be a defining moment in the lives of many Winnebago County residents. Yet, its ultimate legacy is a decidedly mixed one. Some who experienced the decade of despair acknowledged the hard times but appeared to have taken it in stride. Some even looked back at the Thirties with a degree of nostalgia, even exhilaration, and with the conviction that, despite real hardship, these were the good times. Still, others seemed so scarred by the experience of the decade as to shun any reflection or discussion of the time. Perhaps, then, the rather florid, pugilistic metaphor of one observer of the Great Depression in Winnebago County can serve as a fitting conclusion: "The depression aimed mighty blows...had it hanging on the ropes at times...but never down and certainly never licked."[4]

Notes

1. *Oshkosh Northwestern*, December 30, 1939.
2. Michael Goc, *Oshkosh at 150*, p. 173; Steve R. Langkau, *A History of the City of Oshkosh Sanitation Department*, p.14; Steven B. Karges, *Neenah-Menasha Wisconsin and the Great Depression*, p. 124.
3. Steve R. Langkau, *A Thumbnail History of Former City of Oshkosh Industrial Firms*, p. 133.
4. John Miner, "Two Decades of Oshkosh Progress, Despite Odds," p. 3.

INDEX

A
Aid to Dependent Children's Law 4
American Fed. of Labor (AFL) 44, 102
    and Millmen's Local, (1363) 100
    William Green, Pres. 101
American Legion (Oshkosh),
    and unemployment 15
Angermeyer, Howard
    on unemployment 32
Anti-Prohibitionists 48
Atheneum, The 95
    see Raulf, Conrad

B
Badger Lumber Co. 6, 72
    and labor relations 101-02
Bank of Menasha
    re-opening of (1933) 42
Biemiller, Andrew J.,
    Milwaukee Assemblyman and
    labor supporter 99
Bishop, Effie R.,
    Neenah Poor Commissioner 25
    Neenah Red Cross Dir. 25
Black Thursday 1
Bleyer, A.M.
    Dir., Oshkosh Vocational School,
    and unemployed 22
boosterism 52
bootleggers 48
Briggs, Alfred
    Dir., Wisc. Unemployment
    Relief 71
Brown, Taylor, Mayor of Oshkosh
    and municipal gov't. 34
    declines federal relief 58
    ice fishing as survival means 26
    Lakeshore Improvement Proj. 62
Bureau of Family Services 11, 22

C
Campbell, William S.,
    Mayor of Neenah 92
Citizens' Comm. on Unemployment
    12-13, 17
    equalizing unemployment 14
Civil Works Administration (CWA)
    (see FERA)
    and Oshkosh 64-65

and Menasha 64-65
establishment of (1933) 56
national criticism of 72
results in Winnebago Cty. 65-68
Civil Works Service (CWS) 66
Civilian Conservation Corps (CCC)
    camps 44-45, 73
    and education 45
    established by Roosevelt 44
    recreation programs 45
Clarke, J.L., Oshkosh manufacturer 6
Commons, John R.,
    Prof. Labor Econ. UW,
    on unemployment 14
Crash of 1921 6
Crash of 1929 1ff
Crowe, C.F.
    on Crash of 1929 6

D
Diamond Match Co.
    labor relations 101
    operation during Depression 58
Drum, Hugh A.
    and CCC recreation programs 45

E
Eighteenth Amendment,
    repeal of 46
Emergency Conservation Work Act,
    and establishment of CCC 44
Emergency Relief and Construction
    Act (ERCA) 32
    and La Follette 33
Emergency Relief Approp. Act 56
Engelke, Theodore,
    Asst. Sup.,"Hotel Depression" 33

F
Fechner, Robert
    V.P., AFL (1914) 44
    Dir. CCC 44
Federal Art Project 84
Federal Emergency Relief Admin.
    (FERA) 55-57
    and Neenah 58
    and Menasha 58
    Wisc. cities decline aid 57

Federal Labor Relations Board (FLRB) 102
Federal Reserve System 6
Federal Theatre Project 75
Federal Writers Project. 75
Fellenz, Louis T.,
   contender, 6th Dist Congressional seat 35
First Lutheran Church, Oshkosh,
   and recovery 31
First National Bank of Menasha,
   re-opening of (1933) 43
Fleming, Bryan,
   architect of Paine mansion 50
Forbes Magazine,
   on recovery 18
Ford Motor Car Co. 5
Foster, Carlton,
   Chair, Committee on Civic Unemployment 15
Foster, Edith,
   Wisc. Industrial Comm. 33

G
Gabbert, Arthur H.,
   Oshkosh Chief of Police 61, 103
   and Bonnie and Clyde 61
Gaylord, George,
   Pres., Menasha Prod. Co. 31
Genal, Chris M.,
   saloonkeeper and contractor 62-63
Gerhart, Francis,
   Wisc. Match Co. strikes 101-102
Gilbert, Arnold,
   Head, Natl. Farm Holiday Assoc. 104
Great Depression, The, 20, 25, 29-31, 107-108
   and crime 69
   erodes American culture 74
Green, William,
   Pres. AFL 101-102
Grimes, William,
   Wisc. State Assemblyman, 39-40
Gross National Product (GNP)
   1920 7
   1933-37 89

H
H.P. Schmidt Milling Co. 15
Haas, Francis J., Rev.,
   Oshkosh labor supporter 100
Hagene, Henry,
   on unemployment 14
   Lakeshore Improvement Proj. 62
   Oshkosh municipal gov't. 34
Harper, Carl A., Dr.,
   and Oshkosh water 79
Held, W.E.,
   Mayor of Menasha 11
Hemmersley. Charles, 16-17
   election of 1933 13
hoboes,
   on freight trains 42
   accommodated in Neenah jail 16
   Soo Line railroad yard 24
   in Fox Valley 62
Hoover, Herbert, Pres. 2, 5, 11-12,
   and voluntarism 15
Hopkins, Harry,
   and FERA 55
   and WPA 75
   demobilization of Fed. work programs (1934) 66
"Hotel Depression," (Good Will Home) 33, 61
Howman, Louis J. 39
   Supervisor, Outdoor Relief for Winnebago County. 59

I
Ickes, Harold,
   Dir., PWA 56

J
Janda, Frank 23
   labor leader 59,63
Jedwabny, John
   and WERA 30
Jeske, Clarence,
   Secy., Oshkosh Unemployed Council 63
Jones, Wesley C., Senator 49
   Jones Law 48
   amendment to Volkstead Act 49
Jung, Henry,
   Chair, Wisc. Citizen's Comm. on Unemployment 21
Jungwirth, Clarence 62, 94

Index

K
"Kaiser-brew",
    and prohibition 47
Keefe, Frank B.,
    V.P. Oshkosh Bldg & Loan 12
Kennedy, Joseph P., 2
Kerley, Raymond A.,
    and printing business 74
Kimberly-Clark Corp., 57
    labor relations 98
Koch, E.A., Rev. 31
Kohler, Walter, Gov.,
    election of (1930) 12
Kraft, Lawrence,
    Oshkosh music educator 34

L
Laemmele, Carl,
    Hollywood producer 29
La Follette, Philip,
    and Unempl. Comp. Act 29
    election of 1930 13, 17
    Gov. of Wisc. 21
    and Emergency Relief Act 30
La Follette, Robert,
    Gov., Wisc. 13
Lescohier, Donald,
    Prof., Labor Econ. UW.,
        on unemployment 17
Livingstone, John,
    Oshkosh arts organizer 95
"Loan Your Job a Week" 14
Luddism 14
lumber industry,
    decline of 108

M
Malone, Murt
    Superintendent, Oshkosh Pub.
    Employ. Service 5
Meigher, J.W.,
    Pres.,Village of Winnecone,
        Fed. Grants for water
        projects 92
Menasha,
    "City of Paper and Pails..." 3
Menasha Wood Split Pulley Co. 11
Menasha Woodenware Co. 31, 73

Meyer, William A.,
    Mayor of Oshkosh 18
Moore, Franklin,
    opponent of labor unions 102
Morgan Company 50, 72
Mosely, George Van Home,
    CCC activities in southern US 45
Mulholland, E.P.,
    Dir., CCC work programs 45
Mwke. Federated Trades Council 2

N
Nat'l. Ind. Recovery Act (NIRA),
    (1935) 56
    (See PWA)
National Labor Relations Act (NLRA),
    passage of 96
    Wagner Act 96
National Manufacturers' Bank,
    re-opening of (1933) 42
Neenah State Bank,
    re-opening of 42
New Deal,
    and paper contracts 49
    culture of 94
Novotny, Ray,
    Dem., State Assembly 35

O
Oaks, George,
    City Councilman, Menasha,
        and unemployment 14-15
    Mayor of Oshkosh 71
    City Commissioner 62
O'Malley, Thomas J.,
    Acting Gov. of Wisc., (1933)
    and bank closings 42
Oshkosh All Stars,
    NBL championship (1942).
Oshkosh Brewing Company,
    and prohibition 49
Oshkosh Building & Loan Assoc.,
    and recovery 12
Oshkosh Comm. Welfare Fund 35
Oshkosh Millwork Company,
    and recovery 32
Oshkosh Northwestern, The
    and Ford Motor Co. 5
    and millworkers' strike 99

on Crash of 1929 2, 11-12
on CWA experience 71
on effects of Depression 75
on recovery efforts (1931) 26;
    (1932) 35; (1937) 85
on resolution of strikes 96-98
Oshkosh Recreation Dept. 4-5
Oshkosh Truck Co.,
    armaments production 108
Oshkosh West High School *vi*

P

Paine, Charles,
    leadership of Paine Lumber Co. 50
Paine Lumber Co.,
    CCC contracts 72
    closing of (1935) 73
    major regional employer 90
    operation in Depression Era 58
    return to operation (1937) 73
Paine mansion 51
Paine, Nathan,
    Pres. Paine Lumber Co. (1927) 50
Paine Thrift Bank,
    closure of (1933) 41
Peterson, Florence 58-60
    Asst. Secy., Wisc. Citizen's
    Comm. on Unemployment 22
    and relief effort 35
Poe, Alfred E.,
    Industrial Comm. Field Rep.,
        recovery assessment 91-92
Polley, Henry F.,
    Dir., "Hotel Depression" 33
Prohibition 46
Prohibition Act,
    repeal of 46
    1851 referendum 47
    and Presbyterian General
        Assembly 47
Public Works Administration (PWA)
    (see NIRA)
    creation of 56
Public Works of Art Proj. (PWAP) 84

Q

R

Radford Mill (Radford-Wright Plant),
    labor relations 102
Radford, William,
    and Radford Co. 51
Rasmussen and Sons,
    CWA highway contract 64
Raulf, Conrad,
    Oshkosh builder 95
Red Cross
    Midwest branch,
        allocations to Menasha 25
    Menasha Chapter 24
Reilly, Michael K.,
    Congressman, 6th Dist. 35
Remmel, N.G.,
    Mayor of Menasha 22
    and poor relief (1934) 55;
    (1937) 89
Republic Steel,
    strike at Chicago plant 96
Reul, Father William A. 15
"Roosevelt Depression" 92
Roosevelt, Franklin D.,
    popularity of (1932) 33
    election of (1932),
        effect on Wisc. politics 33
    establishment of CCC 43
    inauguration of (1933) 42
Roosevelt, Theodore,
    and conservation 44

S

Sande, George, Mayor of Neenah
    and poor relief 55
    and Wisc. Citizens' Comm. on
        Unemployment 21, 24
"Sawdust City" (Oshkosh) 3, 98, 108
Schmedemann, Albert J.,
    Mayor of Madison 35
    defeat of Kohler 35
    Gov. of Wisconsin 40
    inauguration of (1933) 39
Schurz, Carl,
    and conservation movement 43
    U.S. Secy. of Interior 43
Senn, Roland,
    editor 36-37
        on relief effort 63
Sensenbrenner, John
    Poor Comm., Oshkosh 60

Index   *115*

Shattuck, S,F.
    on labor unrest 97
Sigman, David, AFL organizer
    Diamond Match Co. strike 102
Singler, Walter M.,
    Wisc. Co-op. Milk Pool 41
Skole, James,
    City Comm. (Oshkosh) 26
speakeasies 48
strikes,
    machine industry 98
    milk industry 40 ff
    steel industry 96
    woodworking industry 98

T
Tiedje, August ,
    labor union president 102
Thom, Margaret,
    Dir., Winnebago Cty. Board of Supervisors 25

U
U.S. Govt. Depts. (and CCC)
    Dept. Labor 45
    Dept. Ag. & Interior 45
    Forest Service 44
    War Dept. 45

V
Volkstead Act 48
    violations of 61
    amendment of 49
Volkstead, Andrew
    U.S. Congressman, MN 48
"voluntarism" 15

W
Wagner Act 96
    see NLRA

"Walkathon",
    Raulf's weekly 95
Weber, Frank J.,
    Gen. Secy. Mwke. Fed. Trades Council 2
White, Merritt F.
    Wisc. State Senate 35
Wiechering, Charles A.

Mayor of Oshkosh 99
Pres., Oshkosh City Council 72
and strike resolution 99
and recovery assessment 91
Wisc. Anti-Saloon League 47
Wisc. Axle 6
    response to Crash of 1929 98
Wisc. Brewers' Assoc. 47
Wisc. Coop. Milk Pool 41
Wisc. Emergency Relief Agency (WERA) 58
Wisc. Fed. of Labor 63
Wisc. Industrial Comm., 8, 33
    and WERA 58
Wisc. League of Municipalities 72
Wisc. Match Co.,
    (see Diamond Match Co.)
    labor relations 101
Wisc. Milk Pool 41
Wisc. State Teacher's College (Oshkosh) 82
Woods, Arthur,
    Chair, Fed. Emergency Comm. for Employment 21, 26
Works Projects Admin. (WPA)
    and Menasha 78-79
    and Neenah 78-79
    and Oshkosh 80-82
    effect on American culture 95
    former Works Progress Admin. 56
    "Repair and Improve" 81
Wrabetz, Votya
    labor board member 100

X

Y

Z

www.ingramcontent.com/pod-product-compliance
Lightning Source LLC
Chambersburg PA
CBHW021131300426
44113CB00006B/379